My Intel Story
from the start with Robert Noyce and Gordon Moore till the 50th Anniversary

****

My related books

(Italian) – "La mia storia con Intel" … https://amzn.to/2O8i87K

(Italian) Con Olivetti e Intel, 20 anni di crescita felice e … la fine nel 1987 –   https://amzn.to/2AHQg9h

(Italian) "La mia incredibile avventura marketing con Alan Sugar 1987- 1990" -   https://amzn.to/2uXSprr

(Italian) "Il mostriciattolo semimetallico che ha cambiato il mondo … e il suo cammino dal 1947 al 2050" https://amzn.to/2vtxJre

(English). "The Semimetallic Monsterling that changed our World"   https://amzn.to/2ADcmtD

****

My other English books of possible interest:

Series: Mastering Science for Everybody. https://bit.ly/3UkiDzF

Astrophysics. https://bit.ly/41gM8EA

Einstein: Special relativity. https://bit.ly/3GuluQM

Einstein: General relativity. https://bit.ly/3GzReUE

Quantum Mechanics World. https://bit.ly/40YogGd

Microchip World. https://bit.ly/41OQboI

****

MY INTEL STORY

from the start with Robert Noyce and Gordon Moore till the 50th Anniversary

Series: Tech unlocked for everybody. https://bit.ly/435UyjQ

Paperback Color edition: https://bit.ly/400uELx

Ettore Accenti

Author's news

Linkedin: Ettore Accenti
Blog: http://bit.ly/1qZ9SeK

DISTIWORLD PUBLISHING

Ettore Accenti

My Intel Story from the start with Robert Noyce and Gordon Moore till the 50th Anniversary

Serie: Marketing is fighting 1

English Edition - B/W (rev. Jan 26, 2019)

ISBN-13: 9781729337721

Copyright © 2019 DISTIWORLD PUBLISHING

Dedication

This book is dedicated to Intel and to all of its exceptional people who taught me everything I know about the technology business. In particular, I would like to remember Robert Noyce and Gordon Moore with whom in 1970 I visited initial prospective Italian clients. I owe a lot to Jens Paulsen, Bob Graham, Mike Markkula, Ed Gelbach, Bill Davidow, Tom Lawrence, Stan Mazor, Ted Hoff, Dave House, Hal Feeney, Hank O'Hara, Jack Carsten, Dick Clover and Dov Frohman, all Intel managers that I quote in this book.

A special thanks to Dane Elliot (Historian and Intel Alumni Board Member) for his irreplaceable suggestions and the great help in the correction of the text and the encouragement to publish it.

Sommario

About the author 9

Premise 11

Everything started with an English letter................................. 21

1969. A Daring Meeting 25

I become an Intel partner... 29

1970. Partnership with Intel... 33

1970. Intel Executives 43

Project Shift Register (Ted Hoff) 53

Project RAM 1102/1103 1024 bit 59

1970. Other Intel Data Sheets 75

1971. My two marriages: Eva and Intel 81

Following years with Intel 91

The Rise of Intel Business 97

The quartz watch: An Intel disaster...................................... 105

A gigantic Olivetti Order... 109

Marisa Bellisario visit Intel 115

Intel and the Systems 121

32-bit CPU: the disastrous iAPX432 139

"Crush Program": a masterpiece of marketing..................... 145

The success of the Crush Program at Olivetti ... but! 155

Olivetti-Intel, failed joint venture 161

1991. Meeting with Dr. Gordon Moore and more...................................167

1993 - From the 25th Intel event 177

Conclusion 191

About the author

Lived the technological period from the birth of the Transistor to the integrated circuits and artificial intelligence. Graduated with a degree in electrical engineering at the Polytechnic of Milan. Founded Eledra 3S, a technological distribution company, while still a student. In November 1969, I became the first Intel representative in Europe and lived firsthand through the early Intel period. Ettore Accenti worked with Bob Noyce, Gordon Moore, Mike Markkula, Ed Gelbach, Bill Davidow, Jack Carsten, and many others until 1987. In 1987 he lost his company through a disastrous partnership with the Italian company Olivetti. Following that unfortunate event, he restarted his business life from scratch by founding the Italian subsidiary of Amstrad Plc, a UK Company. In 1991 he became Vice-president at the world headquarters of Memorex-Telex, in charge of world distribution. Since 1997, based in Switzerland, he operates as a consultant, helping companies with their international development, writes technical and economic articles for publication important magazines and self publishes technology books.

Premise

After meeting an Intel executive in 1969, I became the first Intel representative in Europe.

This encounter completely changed my life, and this is the reason that I consider this the best period of my entrepreneurial life, collaborating with Intel for almost 20 years.

I founded my start-up when I was a university student just a couple of years before I graduated with a modest amount of money, but with lots of hope and hard work. In twenty years, that tiny company reached the position of number one in the industrial distribution of electronics products in Italy but, unfortunately, I lost my company in 1987 due to an unfortunate partnership with the Italian company Olivetti.

Despite what happened to my company I continued to deal with the technological world and I am pleased to be able to bring this contribution on the occasion of the 50th anniversary of the foundation of Intel through writing this book.

I will document the wonderful period on which I have been close to Intel by quoting the special people I met including Robert Noyce, Gordon Moore, and many others. This book includes many documents and photos I collected during that period which are contained in my library.

I'm telling my actual story and how it all began in a quite adventurous way. I hope that what I describe may be a lesson for those young entrepreneurs willing to start their own business. I would like to stress how it is important to fight to achieve one's own goals without giving up in the face of difficulties.

Thanks to my detailed recollections and collected documentation, I can connect the facts with the many photos from over 200 photo albums from my library and provide here a historically correct and detailed story.

Going over my calendars, full of annotations, I found a goldmine of information that I had forgotten, and only now can I connect in an orderly manner, reconstructing events relating to the first Intel steps into the market.

My calendars whose content this book is based on

Premise

A picture of my 10,000 pages of stories

I could read my many meetings in Mountain View, in Santa Clara, in Milan and to rediscover the many Intel people who have been visiting Italy at that early Intel time.

My library containing over 200 photo albums, part of which is used here

I collected the beautiful early technical documents beginning in November 1969 that Intel had been publishing, some of which are part of the images shown in this book.

I suppose that many of these documents are no longer available and I hope they can contribute to the historical knowledge of Intel.

In Italy, we created Data Books using the original Intel documents and they are a complete source of technical information that I have partly used here.

In the first 7 years of existence, Intel produced over 2,000 pages of technical documents that are contained in these Data Books, now the best testimony of what, in a few years, Intel was able to achieve.

1977. Collection of Intel data sheets and application notes printed in Italy

In my archive, I keep these nice-looking original binders that were distributed to customers beginning in 1969. They consist of datasheets and application notes describing Intel products and how to use them.

These very elegant documents are distinguished by their beautiful blue with the "Intel" brand in white.

Premise

1969-1970. Detailed and comprehensive product specifications

1970 - Folder for datasheets distribution

16   My Intel Story

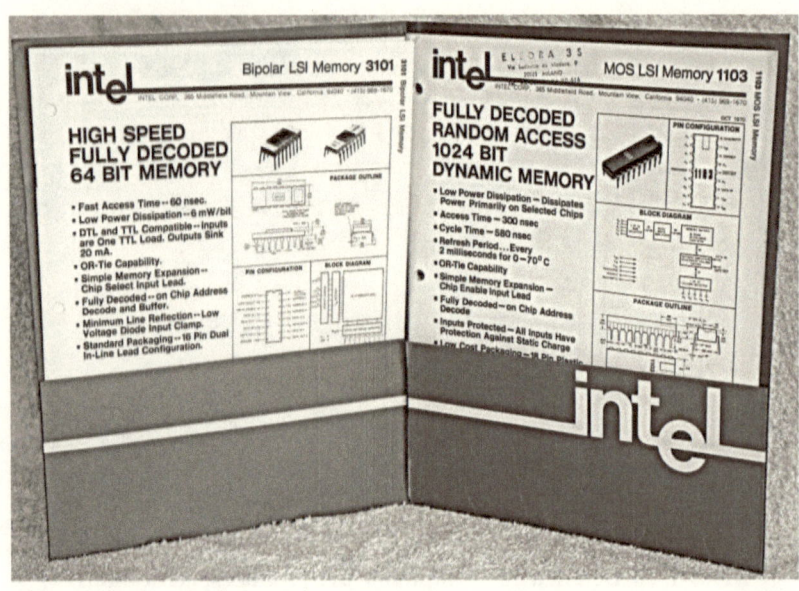

Intel has produced many other nice merchandising items that I found in my archive, such as these two stickers.

I should also confess that I still jealously keep the ashtray made by Intel in 1974 to commemorate the first quarter of sales of more than $ 30 million ... and I believe that this ashtray is unique now.

March 1974 - Intel ashtray ... when to smoke wasn't a crime!

March 1974 – the backside of the Intel ashtray

A gigantic and heavy wood clock carved from a Californian sequoia stands at a wall in my studio reminding me of my Intel tenure. This wonderful gift was given to me while in Santa Clara by Ed Gelbach and Tom Lawrence on the occasion of my fifth year of representing Intel in Italy.

Premise

It was November 1975 and, when I left for my return trip to Italy, I had a lot of difficulties getting it on the plane, but when it reached home safely it was received enthusiastically by my wife Eva.

1975 – Californian Sequoia wood clock. Gift from Intel

Santa Clara March 1979: international distributors conference. On that occasion, Intel gave an Award to the best distributors who made multi-million dollar sales in 1978.

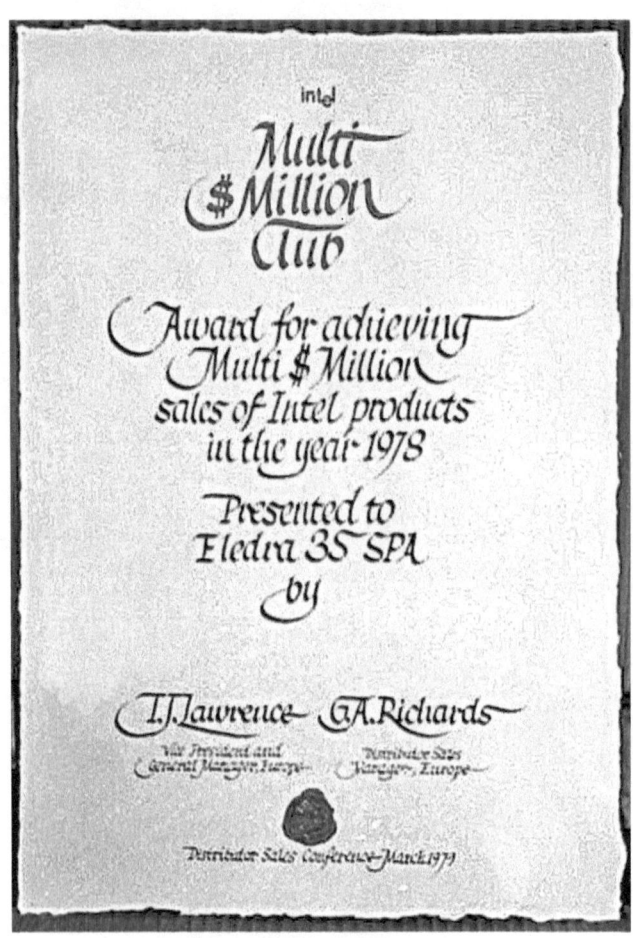

1979 - Distributor Award

Everything started with an English letter

August 7, 1969 – Milan, Ludovico da Viadana 9 street, downtown was my first office. It was a single room, business office and it was a hot summer day.

I could not go on vacation because I was in the final part of my military service at the Air Force headquarters in Milan.

Il My first business offica. Milan, Ludovico da Visdana 9, 700 sqf

I founded my company before starting military service and while attending my fifth year of engineering at Milan Polytechnic.

I called my company "Eledra 3S". The "3S" meant "Solid State Specialties", an area of technology about which I had published many articles and that I enjoyed a lot.

Thanks to the fact that I was performing my military service in Milan, not far away from my office, I could still attend to my business but obviously in a very limited way.

Milan, 1969. While I was performing my military service

Three years earlier I had met my wife, Eva, during a language course in London. We were both residents of Milan and we often spent our free time together.

On that August 7, we had lunch in one of the few restaurants open downtown and after lunch, I proposed to go to my little office that was very close.

I do not know what Eva thought about my proposal, but sincerely I had to hurry up some correspondence before returning to my barracks. I thought to take advantage of Eva's English, which was much better than mine, to write some letters to my UK business contacts.

After finishing with my correspondence to the UK, I decided to write a letter to the US.

A few days before, as a regular reader of American magazines, I read in "Electronics Magazine" news indicating that two of the founders of Fairchild Semiconductor, namely Robert Noyce and Gordon Moore had left Fairchild and founded a new company named Intel in Mountain View, California.

Everything started with an English letter

Palo Alto, August 2, 1968. First press news about the founding of Intel

San Jose, August 6, 1968. Second press news about the founding of Intel

The articles said that Intel stood for INTegrated ELectronics and "integrated electronics" was exactly my main interest as indicated by my company brand "3S" (Solid State Specialties).

I decided to spend some more time at the office writing a letter in English to this new company. I still remember how much time Eva and I spent searching the exact wording and how many times we rewrote that letter to finally reach an acceptable format.

In writing now, Eva reminds me of my bad behavior at that time that I just do not remember.

It seems, that my temporary secretary folded the letter, stuffed it, and glued the expensive stamp by airmail upside down. Eva, still angry, remember that I considered this mistake a "crime" and that I rebuked her bitterly.

According to her, I acted like a surly office manager struggling with a novice clerk and not with someone who was helping me on a Sunday on which she hoped for something better.

Anyhow, as far as for what happened later, I can assure you that the letter reached the destination despite the upside-down the stamp and with great effectiveness.

Two months elapsed with no answer have been received and I regrettably dismissed the idea of collaborating with Intel.

But just when I was sure I had lost the investment of the upside-down stamp, suddenly, at the beginning of November a Mr. Jens Paulsen called me from Geneva, Switzerland, and introduced himself as the newly appointed European manager for Intel.

He had my letter and was just back from a visit to Mountain View where he had accepted his new job. He asked me if I was still interested! I almost fainted.

I assured him that Intel was extremely interesting to me and he added that he would call me back for a meeting in Milan to be held soon.

1969. A Daring Meeting

I read on my calendar about a second phone conversation with Jens Paulsen dated November 7th in which we agreed to meet in Milan at my office on November 13th at 3.30 pm.

That news was a dream becoming true, but now I was faced with the need to convince Jens about my capability to handle the Intel product line. Jens Paulsen would certainly visit other companies in Italy and compare them with my tiny company.

In Italy, there were very well-organized companies distributing American companies with large offices, salesmen, warehouses, etc. etc.

I could not compete with those organizations: my office consisted just of a room with two desks and a table, a bathroom, a corridor, a pre-bath used as a warehouse, a part-time salesman (myself), and a part-time secretary (Eva). More importantly, I, as the owner, salesman, and boss, was still under military service.

Nevertheless, I badly wanted to represent Intel and I had to invent some clever tricks to be successful in convincing Mr. Paulsen!

At the moment I had just the "3S" in the brand name of the company meaning "Solid State Specialties", an evident proof of my specialization, but far from being enough.

No other representative organization in Italy had that specialization, but they could show their history, salesman, warehouse, etc.

Think and rethink, I decided to implement the following strategy: I invented two co-founders of my Eledra 3S, a couple of

Italian elderly industrialists. I succeeded in convincing the father of a classmate of mine, Dr. Guido Giacomini (a steel industrialist) and a friend of his, another well-known industrialist, Dr. Guido Vezzoli, to participate in the meeting with Paulsen.

Their role would have been just that of answering to any financial question Mr. Paulsen could have asked and to confirm the immense financial capability of our company.

My desk at my first office

They did not know any English and I had verified over the phone that Paulsen did not know any Italian, so I would be translating their answers most appropriately during the meeting.

Everything was ready for that Thursday, November 13: Jens Paulsen would have reached us by taxi, and the three of us, the aged industrialists and myself, would have welcomed and discussed the representation of Intel in Italy.

I must say that, despite all these maneuvers at the limit of the ridiculous, the meeting took place and everything went smoothly as planned. During the meeting, I realized that I knew better than Paulsen the semiconductor sector from the scientific standpoint and the newborn semiconductor memories.

As far as the insidious questions about customers, turnover, and salesmen, I did my best to invent as much as I could.
The two industrialists confirmed, through my translation, that any financial need to develop the Intel market would be satisfied. The meeting ended with big handshakes and a "let see you again soon".

Everything seemed OK to me, but it was not so. Soon Paulsen would discover other much more important companies.

I had the impression that our meeting in Milan could be considered a success, but I received a very kind call from Paulsen stating that while he appreciated my great technological knowledge, really amazing, he added that he was looking for a salesman not a professor of physics.

I must say that I was very upset, but not demoralized, I did not accept his conclusion.

I do not remember what I answered exactly at that moment but Jens, with whom I became a friend, later on, explained to me why he changed his mind.

With my poor English, I told him that I did not care about any of his decisions, I would handle the Intel products anyway, even buying them, if necessary, on the free market and that he would never stop me.

After my aggressive response, astonished, he ended the call without denying me a chance and stating that he would have passed my message to Intel. He would let me know the answer in a short time.

I had not won yet, but at least I had stopped his choice toward selecting another organization.

A couple of days later he called me back with the following proposal: "Intel authorizes me to grant you a three-month trial period based on a letter of intent, after which Intel would decide whether to proceed with a regular contract. If it's okay, I'll send you two copies of the letter and you'll have to send me a countersigned copy".

Great! I accepted the proposal with no hesitation, I didn't even ask the content of that letter.

I become an Intel partner

I signed Paulsen's intent letter and a three-month trial period was granted to me after which Intel would decide to proceed with Eledra 3S.

I was confident of succeeding and being able to get substantial sales of those memories within three months. I had already been serving that market niche with Sylvania semiconductors and I knew a handful of clients that could start buying samples of Intel memories.

Sylvania has been my first Semiconductor products representation

I knew that if I could get some orders quickly, the long term representative agreement would be mine.

Long after, I discovered that I had been the first Intel European representative and once I returned the signed letter I received all the available Intel documentation, which consisted of a bunch of technical documents and the first Intel price list dated December 1969. These are documents that I still keep in my archive and which I report here for its historical value.

Dear Sir:

Thank you for your interest in Intel. We have enclosed the product informatin you requested.

The Intel 3101 is a 64 bit random access memory. Its high speed makes it ideal in scratch pad applications.

Intel's 1101 is the first fully decoded 256 bit static MOS RAM. It utilizes a new silicon gate technology which allows much greater component density and circuit performance.

The price breakdown for these circuits is as follows:

1101	Prices
1 - 9 units	$150.00 each
10 - 24 units	$110.00 each
25 - 99 units	$ 80.00 each
100 - 249 units	$ 65.00 each
250 - 499 units	$ 55.00 each

3101	Prices
1 - 9 units	$ 99.50 each
10 - 24 units	$ 74.00 each
25 - 99 units	$ 53.00 each
100 - 249 units	$ 43.00 each
250 - 499 units	$ 38.50 each

Intel circuits are immediately available from your local Cramer Electronics or Hamilton Electro Sales Distributor.

Very truly yours,

R. F. Graham

Robert F. Graham
Director of Marketing

:ss

Enclosures

December 1969 - First Intel price list signed by Robert Graham

A second historical document is the first list of Intel International distributors. In this document, I was quoted along with well-known and larger companies and I must certainly thank Intel for allowing me to be listed among major world distributors.

I become an Intel partner

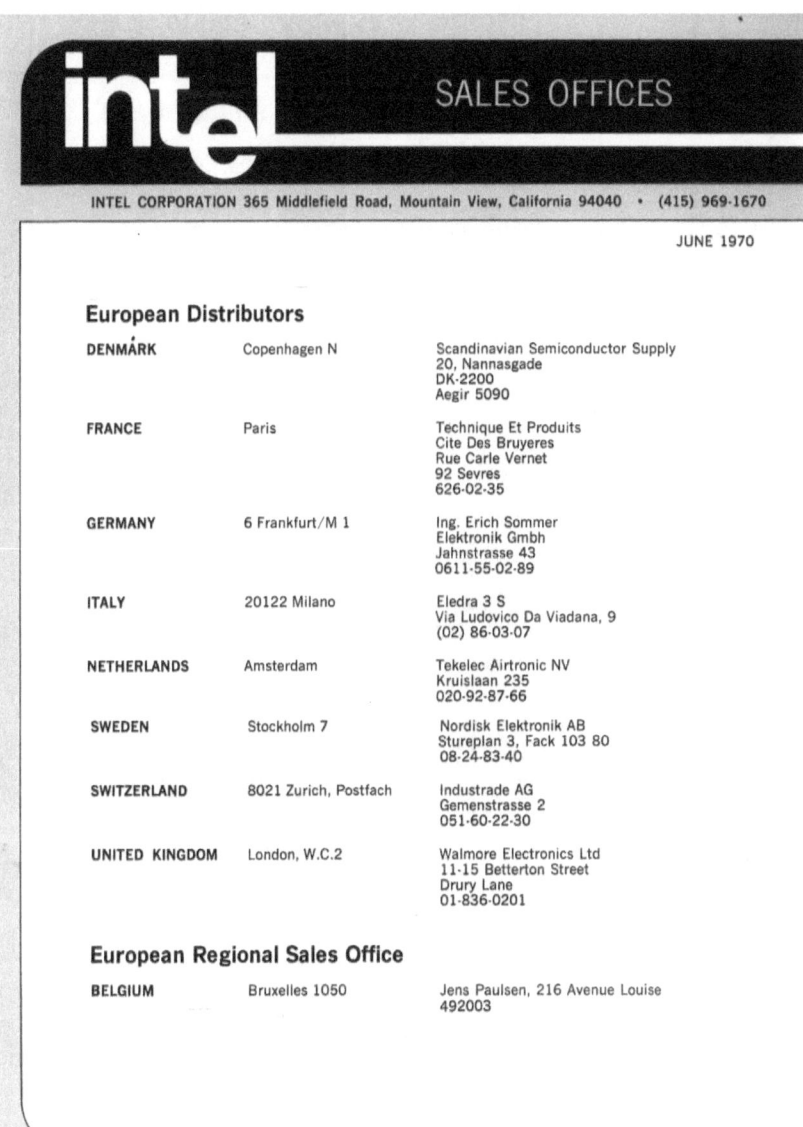

1970 - Official Intel Distributors in Europe

I immediately wrote an article for a technical magazine that was exposed, the first time, semiconductor memories, and the Intel name to the Italian market.

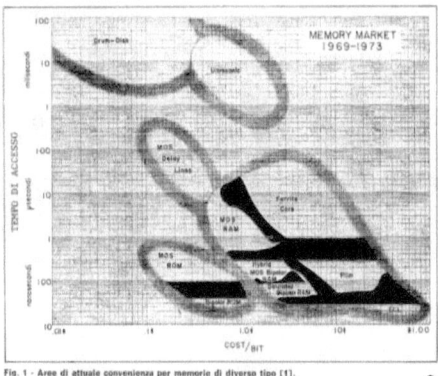

First Italian article about Intel semiconductor memories

By December 1969 I succeeded in selling Intel memories to the laboratories of the Italian subsidiary of General Electric Information Services and IME Spa, an Italian computer company. By December I completed my military service and I could look forward to Intel and my business growing soon after.

1970. Partnership with Intel

My first trip to California started march 2, 1970 leaving for San Francisco from the Malpensa airport. I vividly remember my impressions from that first visit of mine to California: everything seems to me to be very big, roads, hotels, cars, even the hotel room, and the bed.

Palo Alto, my hotel booked by Intel

My first breakfast was incredible. In Italy, I was used to getting just a couple of cookies and a cup of cappuccino: all those foods in front of me, early in the morning, were confusing me, I thought it was a dinner not breakfast.

Nevertheless, I loved the American style so much that I came back to Italy ten days later weighing 5 pounds more than when I left!

As an enthusiast photographer, I took pictures of everything around me, streets, buildings, cars, and my hotel room which was perhaps, larger than my Italian office in Milan.

Palo Alto, the large hotel room at the Cabana Hyatt House

In the morning I left the hotel by car, I turned right and then left into the San Antonio Road. I drove about a mile and then I turned left into the Middlefield Road. A half a mile down the road, on the left, I would see the street number "365". This was where the first Intel building was located.

I could not resist stopping the car, picking up my camera, and taking a few photos of that now historical building.

Being there for the first time I had the feeling of being in some kind of wonderland. For several years I had been reading the name "Mountain View" in American magazines, and that name had become legendary to me as Petra in Jordan or Egyptian Pyramids for an archaeologist.

1970. Partnership with Intel 35

I knew that the Nobel Prize-winning Dr. William Shockley founded "Shockley Semiconductor Laboratory" there and that Fairchild Semiconductor headquarter were there too.

I was aware that not far away was the famous Stanford University and Hewlett Packard, a world technology leader whose products I had the opportunity to study.

My feeling was that I was at the center of what, one day, would be called "Silicon Valley", the most important concentration of technology companies in the world

I can now say: "I was there!" and I witnessed the start of a new world now called the "Digital World".

March 3, 1970 – 365 Middlefield Rd, Mountain View, Intel's first factory

Since then I paid zillions of visits to that area and in the end, I could drive there with more ease than when I was in Milan, my hometown.

At Intel I met Bob Graham, marketing manager, waiting for me in the lobby. I had the honor of being escorted by Bob during my first tour at Intel where he introduced me to the various executives working there

Bob Graham at the entrance to the Intel's facilities

The following day he invited me to his home, not far from the factory where I could meet his wife and his two children.

March 4, 1970 - Bob Graham's house

1970. Partnership with Intel

I met both Dr. Gordon Moore and Dr. Robert Noyce with whom I spend some time with and had few words about my just started Italian business. They both kindly let me know what was going on there, talks that increased my enthusiasm even more for their company.

Noyce informed me about his plan to visit soon Italy and we agreed to meet in Italy shortly after I visited California.

He was conversant about the Italian electronic market thanks to his experience as president of Fairchild, a partner of the Italian "Società Generale Semiconduttori" that he visited many times.

During my visit, I was asked to sign a "non-disclosure agreement", before being informed about new products.

I was impressed with a ROM (Read Only Memory) that could be erased and re-programmed.

This was a wonderful solution for design engineers who could modify their prototypes in their lab without having to wait for the expensive production of new ROMs containing their code.

Dr. Dov Frohman, the inventor of that "thing", showed me how he could erase the content of that chip by passing over it an ultraviolet lamp.

I did not quite, understand what the hell the magic was he was talking about, but then he explained how that memory worked and how he was expecting to solve the problem of developing prototypes quickly.

That component would soon become the EPROM (Erasable Programmable Read-Only Memory) 2048-bit i1702 with which I would go on to sell, with high profits to the Italian laboratories.

Among other people I met there, I remember Les Vadasz, Andy Grove, and Ted Hoff, all engaged in their hard work of creating new products.

The message that came to me strong there was that of speeding up the replacement of the huge magnetic memories market with Intel semiconductor memories.

Intel was then developing a new memory chip that would be cost-competitive with magnetic core memories. It was a 1024 bit memory based on their new silicon-gate technology.

This component, soon labeled i1103, was not yet released but I would start to sell it a few months later.

As agreed during my visit, the first week of April 1970 Robert Noyce flew to Milan, and I picked up him at the airport to start visits we had organized in advance.

Dr. Roberto Olivetti, Olivetti president, was our first contact located in Ivrea and we had lunch with him at the Olivetti factory.

The following day we visited Dr. Virgilio Floriani, president and founder of Telettra and partner of SGS.
While I was driving Noyce around north Italy we talked about various topics concerning Intel's business and I must say that his particular and unexpected cordiality greatly reduced my anxiety in front of such an important person.

On a couple of occasions, he proposed that I joined the Intel staff as an employee, but I did not accept them because I wanted to remain in Italy and continue to work as an independent entrepreneur.

I met Noyce many times in California and during the sales meetings that Intel has been organizing in beautiful locations.
Coming back to the year 1970, in April, I visited both Olivetti and HISI, with Bob Noyce, Ted Hoff, and Jens Paulsen. These meetings

1970. Partnership with Intel

were extremely useful for understanding the Intel policy and the potential business at Olivetti.

I was not used to meeting at such an important level and I was absorbing everything like a sponge.

At the time, my task was limited at taking notes of what was going on and to outline any action to be carried out later on. For instance to supply samples, to provide detailed technical answers, to formalize offers, and to confirm in writing certain important statements.

Those notes are part of my archive and I can report here some of what Intel was forecasting in terms of pricing and technology evolution that was conveyed to Olivetti in 1970.

On April 29, 1970, Noyce announced at Olivetti that the price per bit of dynamic memories would reach 0.8 cents per dollar in 1971 and 1 cent per bit for shift registers.

I noted also that Olivetti informed Noyce about their market that at the moment consisted of 32% accounting machines, 48% calculating machines, and 20% of the latter consisted of numerical controls and data control. Olivetti also added that 65% of their production was exported.

I could never have organized such meetings by myself, on top of that I could not give such authoritative answers.

I understood then how important it was to provide information on the present and also to inform these big clients how the prices will evolution in the future, including the long term.

"Moore's law" established in 1965 was intrinsic this and would be recognized as such only long afterward. This was a new world in which this business belonged with an ever-decreasing price curve for the future.

Companies like Olivetti and HISI had to make choices of how to design products that would not go into production for two or three years, but they had to evaluate their costs immediately, concerning the future.

It was essential to predict the future, but even this was not enough, it was also necessary to have the authority to deliver and credibility was what Intel executive had.

In the nineties, that way of informing the market about future generations of microprocessors, with the relative prices, will be a highly competitive fact for the conquest of the great manufacturers of Personal Computers. This trade policy will help make Intel the great company it is today.

As far as Italy was concerned, the aforementioned merger of General Electric with Honeywell gave rise to HISI, number two in the computer sector after IBM, and consequently, at Pregnana Milanese there was a technological hub of world quality. I read found my calendars contained a lot of news and information referring to that period, almost all of which I had forgotten.

Among the many notes, I think it is important to report here some of the information I recorded from comments by Gordon Moore, Bob Graham, Mike Markkula, and others.

Markkula, who later became the partner and financier of Apple Computer, visited me only once. Later, however, I frequently saw him at the factory in Santa Clara.

Gordon Moore spent a couple of days in Italy, specifically the 24th and 25th of September 1970, during which we visited Olivetti and HISI, extending the efforts made by other Intel executives.

Olivetti made sure many executives attended meetings with Gordon Moore, already considered one of the main experts in semiconductor technology, and well-known author of numerous scientific papers.

1970. Partnership with Intel

Dr. Gordon Moore published what would become "Moore's Law" in his now-famous article in 1965.

Among other participants in these meeting with Olivetti I recorded the presence of De Sandre, Rivara, Santerini, Vittorelli, Muzzani, Ferroglio, Olivi, Mercurio, Subrizi, Locatelli, Ferrari and Bortacci.

To be frank, more than a meeting between supplier and client, I felt these meetings were part of a high-tech course from Stanford University.

The main topic was the recently developed Dynamic RAMs (DRAM) and the expected future development of higher density, faster DRAMs that would continue to lower the cost on a per-bit basis substantially. Dr. Moore answered all of the many questions, even the most insidious ones about the long term future of DRAM technology.

Moore foresaw a 4096 bit-RAM in the fairly near future and confirmed the decreasing price even beyond that device.

He mentioned the sizes of the memory chips that for the 256-bit i1101 confirmed to be 25 square mills and 6.5 square mills for the 1024-bit i1103 chip.

I realized then, how competitive these new dynamic memories were and why Intel was betting so much on them.

The following day we met HISI at Pregnana Milanese where Dr. Moore met with a large group of engineers among whom I recorded the presence of Bentivoglio, Profumo, Gunel, Ruffi, Rondino, Giuliani, Broschi, Pinto, Forlani, Vinsani, Preziosa, Guarnaschelli, and Zuliani. The main topic of the meeting was again (DRAM) dynamic memories and their future costs.

I could not forget what both Gordon Moore and Bob Noyce were telling me while we were driving on the highway between Milan and Turin. While I was driving quite fast and conversing with them I got interrupted and asked to slow down! I didn't know the American way to drive and their speed limits. As I frequently did, I was driving at more than 100 miles per hour!

Apart from my Italian driving style, I had a great opportunity to ask questions about technology and business of them and received a lot of answers again, like being at a high-level tutorial course.

Along the following years of my collaboration with Intel, I met Noyce and Moore many times.

Even after my work at Intel, which ended the year 1987, I visited Silicon Valley many times and continued to greet them as old friends.

In the two chapters that follow I report part of the technical documentation that I collected in that year 1970 and which I jealously kept in my historical archive.

I hope that this material is of particular interest to all those people who are studying that period of Intel.

1970. Intel Executives

The 10 images that I here am reproducing in full were part of the documents that Intel sent to customers in the early 1970s describing the 10 key characters in its management structure.

My Intel Story

1970. Intel Executives

Dr. Grove received his Bachelor of Science degree from the City University of New York in 1960 and his Ph.D. degree from the University of California in 1963.

He subsequently joined the Physics Department of the Research and Development Laboratory, Fairchild Semiconductor, Palo Alto, California. During his five years at Fairchild Semiconductor, Dr. Grove contributed significantly to work that led to major developments in semiconductor technology including:

- Control of surface properties of silicon.
- Stability in MOS devices
- Stability in high voltage PNP transistors
- Very high voltage NPN transistors.

In 1967 he was appointed Assistant Director of Research and Development.

Dr. Grove holds several patents pertaining to surface controlled semiconductor devices. He has written over 30 technical papers on semiconductor devices and technology on subjects which include diffusion, epitaxial growth, thermal oxidation, surface effects and MOS devices, and radiation effects.

He has authored a book used at many leading universities in the United States, **Physics and Technology of Semiconductor Devices**, John Wiley & Sons, Inc. (1967), and is currently teaching a graduate course in semiconductor device physics at the University of California.

Dr. Grove is a member of Tau Beta Pi, the American Physical Society and the IEEE. He has been a member of the Electronic Materials Committee of the American Institute of Metallurgical Engineers and presently serves on the Administrative Committee of the Electron Devices Group of the IEEE.

intel

Dr. Andrew S. Grove
Director of Operations
INTEL CORPORATION/365 MIDDLEFIELD ROAD, MOUNTAIN VIEW, CALIF. 94040

My Intel Story

Mr. Fitzgerald received his Bachelor of Engineering degree from University College, Dublin, Ireland, and his Master of Science degree in Electrical Engineering from Marquette University.

From 1962 through 1969, Mr. Fitzgerald had extensive experience in semiconductor physics and technology at Fairchild Semiconductor. As a member of first the Physics Department and later the Digital Integrated Electronics Department, he worked in the following areas:

- Study of failure mechanisms in both n- and p-channel MOS transistors.
- Investigation of the mechanisms of channel current formation. This work led to the development of the first stable high voltage pnp transistors.
- Investigation of the surface properties of silicon, especially surface recombination velocity. This work led to the development of bipolar transistors having very high current gains at low current levels.
- Development of LSI logic arrays.
- Study of radiation–induced failure mechanisms in bipolar, MOS and junction field-effect transistors.

Mr. Fitzgerald is co-author of 10 technical papers related to semiconductor device physics and failure phenomena.

He is a member of the IEEE and Sigma XI.

Desmond J. Fitzgerald
Manager Quality Assurance
INTEL CORPORATION/365 MIDDLEFIELD ROAD/MOUNTAIN VIEW, CALIF. 94040

1970. Intel Executives

Mr. Flath received his Bachelor of Science degree in Electrical Engineering from the University of Wisconsin and his Master of Science degree in Electrical Engineering from the University of New Hampshire.

After spending four years as a Naval officer, Mr. Flath joined Fairchild Semiconductor as a Production Supervisor and advanced himself to Product Manager of all proprietary integrated circuits. In this capacity he managed wafer fabrication, wafer sort, and finished product test areas for all standard digital integrated circuit families including DTL, CTL, TTL, RTL, LPDTL, MSI and bipolar memory circuits. His group of over 250 people was also responsible for mask design, process development, and sustaining engineering.

Mr. Flath's major contributions at Fairchild include:
- Development of shallow diffused high speed CTL process.
- Directed process improvement of CTL to effect a 300% die sort yield increase over a six-month period.
- Reduced overall cost of manufacturing integrated circuit wafers by 20%.
- Supervised development of masks and process for 20 MSI and complex bipolar memory circuits, including a 64-bit ROM.
- Improved overall digital integrated circuit yields by 50%.

Mr. Flath is a member of the IEEE.

intel
Eugene J. Flath
Manager Wafer Fabrication
INTEL CORPORATION/365 MIDDLEFIELD ROAD/MOUNTAIN VIEW, CALIF. 94040

My Intel Story

1970. Intel Executives

My Intel Story

1970. Intel Executives

Mr. Bohn received his Bachelor of Science degree in Mechanical Engineering and Master of Science degree in Electrical Engineering from Ohio University. He is a member of Tau Beta Pi.
During the past eight years at Transitron Semiconductor, Fairchild Semiconductor and Sylvania Semiconductor, Mr. Bohn has had extensive experience in process development and the design and testing of semiconductor devices including:

- Responsibility for silicon planar transistor development at Transitron including process, specification design and testing.
- Developed processing techniques to begin the Sylvania integrated circuit operation. Designed, processed and characterized TTL logic family. Wrote specifications and helped to establish initial manufacturing capability.
- Participated in the design of DTL logic family at Fairchild Research and Development Lab. Assisted in the specification of the process and transfer to manufacturing.
- Designed, specified and characterized a 1 ns CML logic family operating in a transmission line environment. Wrote an internal paper which relates device design parameters to electrical stability in strip line transmission environments as a function of characteristic impedance, I/O impedance, fanout and positional loading.
- Directed circuit design efforts at Sylvania to develop and manufacture MSI circuits.
- Managed Sylvania LSI and Custom Circuit effort which led to the successful manufacture of 3 layer metal interconnect patterns and 3 ns TTL logic family.

Mr. Bohn is co-holder of a patent covering TTL integrated circuit structures and has written several technical papers relating to design principles for integrated circuits.

Richard E. Bohn
Manager Bipolar Engineering
INTEL CORPORATION/365 MIDDLEFIELD ROAD/MOUNTAIN VIEW, CALIF. 94040

My Intel Story

Project Shift Register (Ted Hoff)

I then collected many original documents illustrating Intel's first steps in the design of memory devices. I'll review a few historical documents. The 1024 bit shift register was Intel's first 1K memory device, long before the 1103 DRAM.

```
                    1408-Quad 64 Bit Accumulator
                    1409-Dual 128 Bit Accumulator
                    1410-256 Bit Accumulator
                          (Rev 1. 4/24/70)
```

DESCRIPTION

The Quad 64-bit accumulator has four (4) recirculating 64-bit shift registers with common read" and "write/recirculate" control. Similarly, the dual 128-bit accumulator has two recirculating 128-bit shift registers and the 256-bit accumulator has a single 256-bit recirculating shift register. They use a 2 phase clock. The circuit is TTL/DTL compatible on the inputs and outputs. The circuits use standard DIP and TO-5 packages.

CHARACTERISTICS

Output Sink Current	≥ 1.6 mA @ $V_{out} = .45V$
Input Logic Levels	
Logic "1"	$\geq + 2.5V$
Logic "0"	$\leq + .45V$
Output Logic Levels	
Logic "1"	$\geq + 2.5V$
Logic "0"	$\leq + .45V$
V_{DD}	$-5V$
V_{CC}	$+5V$
Clock Levels	
High	$V_{CC} +.3\ -1.0V$
Low	$-10 \pm 1.0V$
Temperature Range	$-55°$ to $85°C$
Clock Frequency	2MHz max
Clock Capacitance	≤ 50 pF

PIN CONFIGURATION

1408, 1409, 1410 pin diagrams (Top View)

TIMING DIAGRAM

Input Phase ϕ_2, Output Phase ϕ_1, WRITE, DATA IN, READ, DATA OUT, t_{access}

COMMENTS

Information is written into the accumulator with logic "0" applied to WRITE/RECIRCULATE control. Information will recircuate with logic "1" applied to the WRITE/RECIRCULATE control. Output is at logic "1" if READ is at logic "1". True data will appear at output if READ is logic "0".

ROUGH DRAFT
MEH/mjm/6-18-70

USING STANDARD-LENGTH SHIFT REGISTERS IN CUSTOM-LENGTH APPLICATIONS
M. E. Hoff, Jr.

Standard length shift registers may be used for certain custom length applications if the clock rate of the equivalent custom length shift register need not exceed half the maximum rate of the shift register used.

By storing a given item of data in two successive locations of a shift register, the length of the register is effectively reduced by 1. This double storage may be achieved by clocking the shift register twice for the same data. With two-phase data operations, such as in the 1402,3,4 family, this mode is slightly more difficult to achieve. Nevertheless, the schematic shown permits arbitrary-length shift register operation from members of the 1402,3,4 family. In the figure, it is desired to use the M-bit long collection of shift registers to realize an N bit long equivalent shift register. An address counter equivalent to that used for the N length shift register is used. However, the logic circuit L generates an output which is high for M-N of the states of the address counter (therefore, $N \geq \frac{M}{2}$). For each state of the address counter for which the output of L is high, the shift register is clocked an extra step. Thus, in N steps of the address register, the shift register advances M steps; i.e., one complete circulation. Note that the system clock runs at twice the rate that would be used for normal operation. Note also that data at the shift register must remain stable for the full data period (two cycles of the system clock).

As an example, consider the use of a 512 bit shift register for a 500 bit application. The 500 state address counter must be coupled to a logic circuit which gives a "1" output for 12 of these states. Suppose the address counter consists of the following sequence of counter stages: ÷5, ÷2, ÷5, ÷2, ÷5, and that each ÷5 counter consists of 3 flip flops counting in the sequence 000, 001, 010, 011, 100, 000. If one detects the coincidence of one state (such as the 000 state) from two of the ÷5 counters, for each state of the third ÷5 counter, the first two ÷5 counters will both be in the 000 state

ROUGH DRAFT
Page 2

for four of the 500 states of the full address counter. By combining coincidence of the 000 state in each of the first two ÷5 counters with occurrence of three of the states of the third ÷5 counter, an output is derived which is true for 12 states of the full address counter. The circuit to accomplish this function is shown in Figure 2.

Project Shift Register (Ted Hoff)

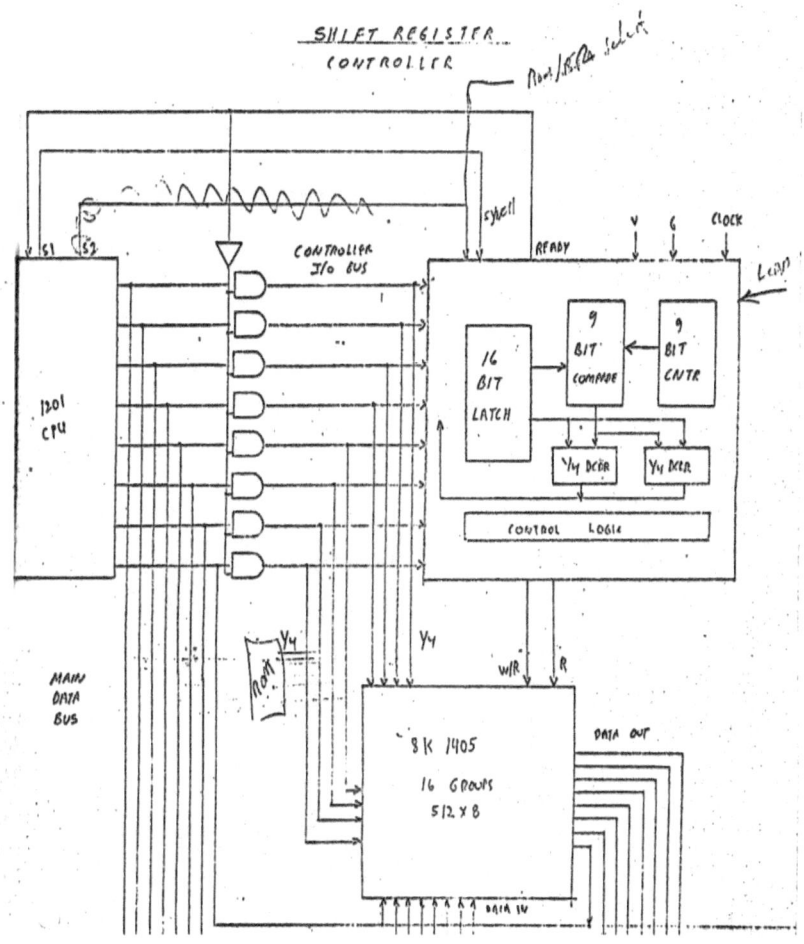

Fogure 1

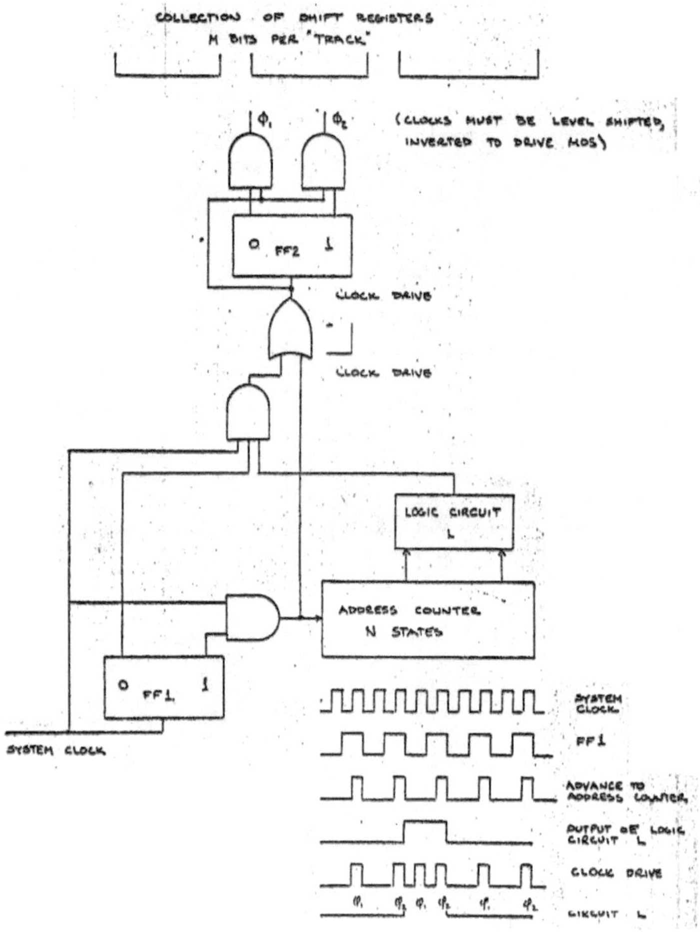

COLLECTION OF SHIFT REGISTERS
M BITS PER "TRACK"

(CLOCKS MUST BE LEVEL SHIFTED, INVERTED TO DRIVE MOS)

FF2

CLOCK DRIVE

CLOCK DRIVE

LOGIC CIRCUIT
L

ADDRESS COUNTER
N STATES

FF1

SYSTEM CLOCK

SYSTEM CLOCK

FF1

ADVANCE TO ADDRESS COUNTER

OUTPUT OF LOGIC CIRCUIT L

CLOCK DRIVE
$\phi_1\ \phi_2\ \phi_1\ \phi_2\ \phi_1\ \phi_2$
CIRCUIT L

Project Shift Register (Ted Hoff)

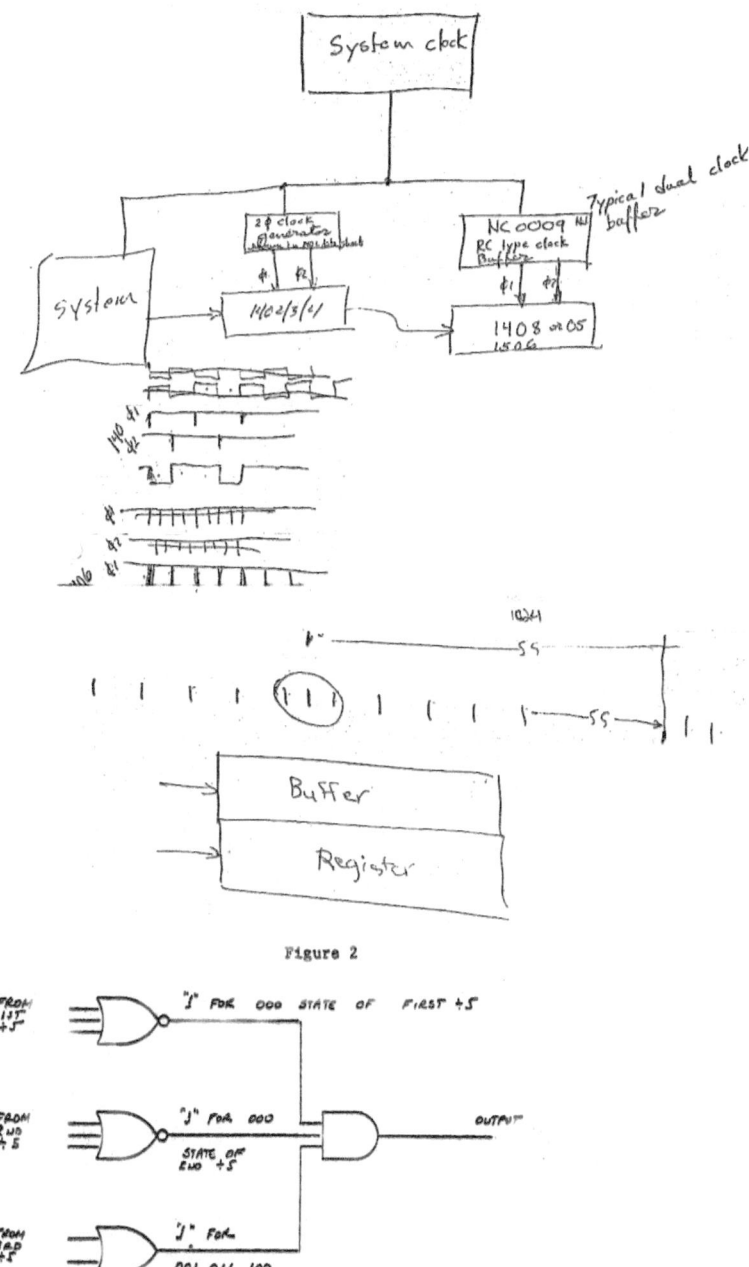

Figure 2

 MOS LSI Shift Register **1406, 1506, 1407, 1507**

INTEL CORP. 365 Middlefield Road, Mountain View, California 94040 • (415) 969-1670

DUAL 100 BIT DYNAMIC SHIFT REGISTER

- Low Power Dissipation--.4 mW/bit at 1 MHz
- High Frequency Operation -- 2 MHz Guaranteed
- DTL, TTL Compatible
- Low Clock Capacitance -- 40 pF
- Low Clock Leakage -- ≤.5 µA at −18 V
- Inputs Protected Against Static Charge
- Standard Packaging -- Low Profile TO-5
- Military and Commercial Temperature Ranges
- Low Output Impedance -- 300 Ω Typical

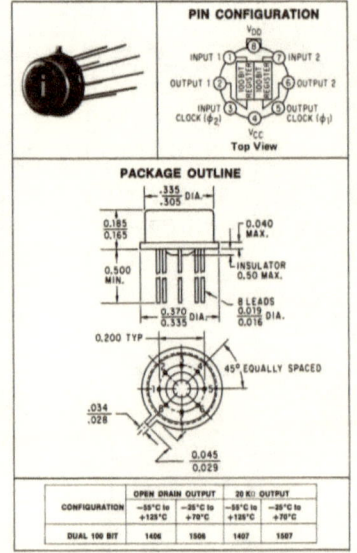

The Intel dual 100 bit dynamic shift register element consists of normally off P-channel MOS devices integrated on a monolithic array. It uses low voltage circuitry to minimize power dissipation and to facilitate interfacing with bipolar integrated circuits. It uses two clock phases only.

The dual 100 bit device can be driven directly by standard bipolar integrated circuits (TTL, DTL, etc.) or by MOS circuits. The design of the output stage provides driving capability for MOS or bipolar IC's.

Use of the low threshold **silicon gate technology** allows high speed (2 MHz guaranteed), while reducing power dissipation by a factor of 2 and reducing clock input capacitance by a factor of 3 compared to equivalent products manufactured by conventional MOS technologies.

This family is designed for low cost buffer applications. It is available in both military (−55°C to +125°C) and industrial (−25°C to +70°C) grade. It is also available with or without an internal 20K pull-up resistor which may provide easier interfacing to other circuitry.

Project RAM 1102/1103 1024 bit

I should acknowledge the competition between 1102 and 1103. The former was designed by Honeywell and 1103 by Intel. 1103 chosen because of its origin and to assure no conflicts on the open market. Both were prototyped by Intel.

PRELIMINARY PRODUCT INFORMATION

i-1102 and i-1103

Some Change

Intel's 1102 and 1103 products are MOS Random Access Memories; each are 1024 bits, fully decoded, in a 18 lead hermetic dip. They use "clocked" logic circuitry to achieve high functional density at high speed and low power dissipation. They are manufactured with silicon gate technology.

They are designed to fit applications where cores were used previously or where the performance of cores is not satisfactory. In the case of the i-1102, it meets the performance characteristics of the highest speed cores available, while the i-1103 is faster than any core memory in existence. Power dissipation is in the few (10-15 μW/bit) microwatt per bit region for each of these products.

In the following, we shall define the comparative characteristics of these two products and their basic principle of operation.

PARAMETER	i-1102	i-1103	COMMENTS
Package	16 Lead DIP	16 Lead DIP	
No. of Bits/Package	1024	1024	
Organisation	512 x 2	512 x 2	
No. of Power Supplies	1	1	
Power Supply Voltage, V_{SS}	+20V ± 5%	+20V ± 5%	The chip is referenced t
Mode of Operation	Clocked, NDRO	Clocked, NDRO	
Temp Range	0 to 70°C	0 to 70°C	
Access Time	250-340 ns	100-150 ns	See "Principle of Operat
Cycle Time	450-500 ns	200-250 ns	Maximum data rate
Clock input "hi" level	$+20^{+.3}_{-1.0}V$	$+20^{+.3}_{-1.0}V$	
"lo" level	$0^{+1.0}_{-1.0}V$	$0^{+1.0}_{-1.0}V$	
Address input "hi" level	$+20^{+.3}_{-1.0}V$	$+20^{+.3}_{-1.0}V$	
"lo" level	$0^{+1.0}_{-1.0}V$	$0^{+1.0}_{-1.0}V$	
Output current	>300 μA ~333~	>300 μA ~333~	Output terminated to GN thru 200 ohm resistor /150/
Address input capacitances	≤5 pf	≤5 pf	@ V in = +20V
Clock input capacitances "PRECH" "XENBL" "YENBL"	≤25 pf ≤10 pf ≤30 pf	≤30 pf ≤10 pf ≤35 pf	
Output capacitance	≤ 5 pf	≤ 5 pf	

Power Dissipation

At this time, we cannot define maximum limits to any better accuracy. Once a product distribution is established, the parameters will be firmly defined.

Clocked (dynamic) MOS circuits work on the principle of storing charge on a capacitor; the process of charging/discharging capacitors is through MOS transistors in some circuit combination.

Consider the circuit of Figure 1 below:

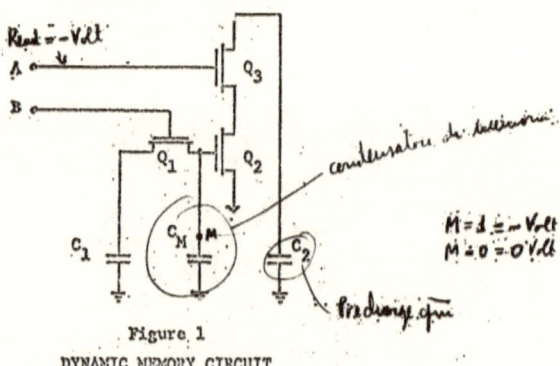

Figure 1
DYNAMIC MEMORY CIRCUIT

The information is stored on capacitor C_M. Negative charge on this capacitor is a logic "1", while no charge on this capacitor represents a logic "0". For a negative charge (logic "1") on C_M, Q_2 will be in its conductive state and for no charge on C_M, Q_2 will be cut off.

The state of the cell can be interrogated by turning transistor Q_3 "on". This is accomplished by applying a negative voltage to point "A" of Figure 1. If capacitor C_2 was precharged to a negative voltage prior to turning Q_3 "on", this charge will now be discharged through Q_2 and Q_3 if C_M stores charge. No charge on C_M will thus result in leaving C_2 charged negative. This, in turn, can be amplified and sensed through some additional MOS circuitry on the chip.

Transistor Q_1 will be used for two purposes:

1. To "WRITE" new information into the memory.

2. To "REFRESH", that is, periodically rewrite the information into the cell. This feature is a basic property of all MOS dynamic memory or logic circuits; the storage node will hold its information for a restricted period of time only. If information is to be maintained, it will have to be refreshed at some time interval. In the present application, the total

Project RAM 1102/1103 1024 bit

time required for refreshing the memory is very small; it adds less than one per cent (1%) to the average access time of the circuit. We shall expand on this point later.

Transistor Q_1 is turned "on" by applying a negative potential to point of Figure 1.

A memory "READ" cycle will be as follows:

1. Precharge C_2 and all necessary logic gates.
2. Decode to point "A" to conditionally discharge C_2.
3. a. Turn "on" Q_1 and refresh information in cell.
   b. Read out data.

A memory "WRITE" cycle will essentially be the same, except instead of refreshing the old information in the cell we WRITE new information using the same bus line as we used for data output (DIGIT) lead.

The circuit has three clocks. These are used for:

1. Precharge (PRECH) the internal bus lines to their proper potential.
2. Enable the X decode circuitry (XENBL) to select an X-line (i.e., point "A" on Figure 1) for read/write/refresh operation.
3. Enable the Y decode circuitry (YENBL) to select a memory position on the already decoded X-line for read or write operation.

The memory organization is shown on Figure 2 on page 5.

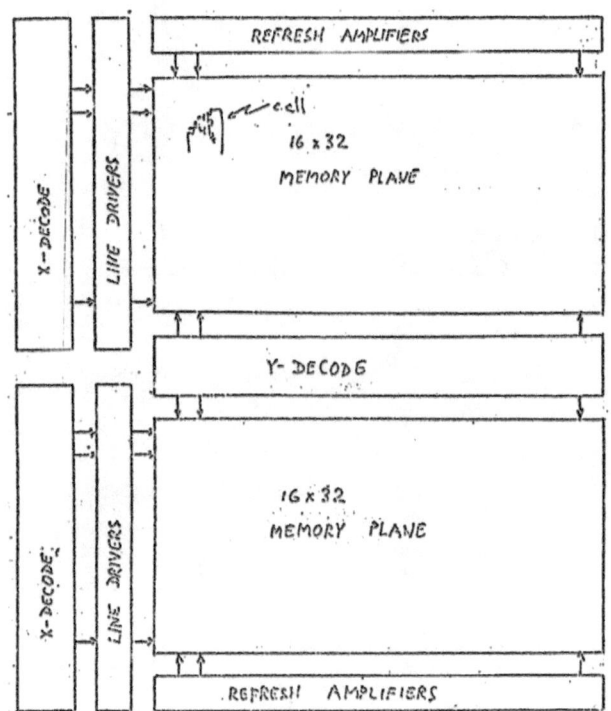

Figure 2.
MEMORY ORGANIZATION

- 5 -

Project RAM 1102/1103 1024 bit

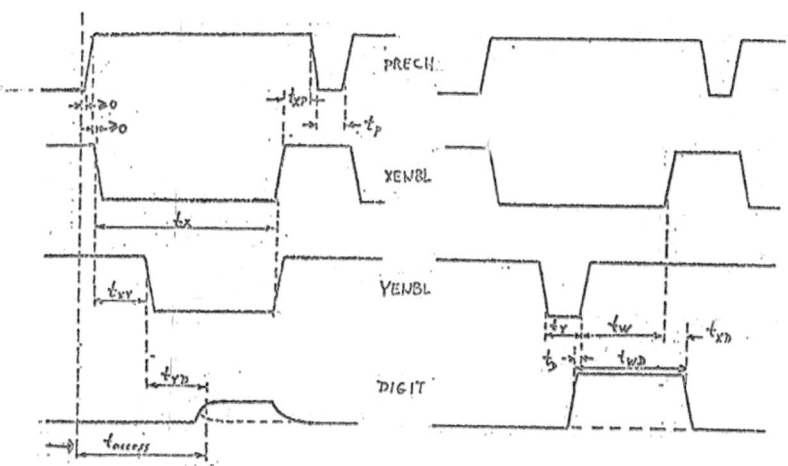

READ TIMING
Figure 3

WRITE TIMING
Figure 4

SYMBOL	PARAMETER	READ TIME (nsec) i-1102	READ TIME (nsec) i-1103	WRITE TIME (nsec) i-1102	WRITE TIME (nsec) i-1103
	XENBL pulse duration	400 min	160 min	400 min	160 min
	YENBL to XENBL pulse delay	200-240 min	60 min	200-240 min	60 min
	YENBL pulse duration			75 min	50 min
	PRECH to XENBL pulse delay	40 min	40 min	40 min	40 min
	PRECH pulse duration	50 min	50 min	50 min	50 min
	Data out to YENBL delay	100 max	70 max		
	Write time			85 min	50 min
D	XENBL to data in overhang			50 min	50 min
	YENBL to data in overlap			≥ 0	≥ 0
ccess	Access time	300-340 max	150 max		
ycle	Cycle time	500 max	250 max	500 max	250 max

All rise and fall times are 20 nsec.

As seen in Figure 4, the only difference between a READ cycle and a WRITE cycle is the time duration of the YENBL clock. The write time, t_W is defined as the time delay between the positive transitions of YENBL and XENBL clocks. Information is written through the DIGIT line. Logic "1" is ~0 V while logic "0" is + 20 V on this line.

INTERFACE CIRCUITRY

Two characteristic features of this memory are high voltage address and clock inputs and the need for a sense amplifier on the output. The circuits we have used for our own experiments are shown below.

a. Driver Circuit

Figure 6 shows the circuit diagram of a typical driver stage. Input voltages are directly from TTL outputs. Level conversion from TTL levels to 20V signals is accomplished in less than 20 nsec. Typical delay through this driver and the output rise and fall times are shown on CRT trace, Figure 6. Note that less than 10 nsec rise and fall times can be achieved with this driver.

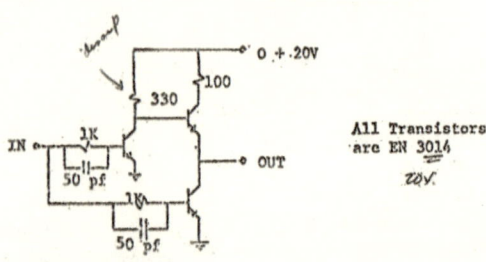

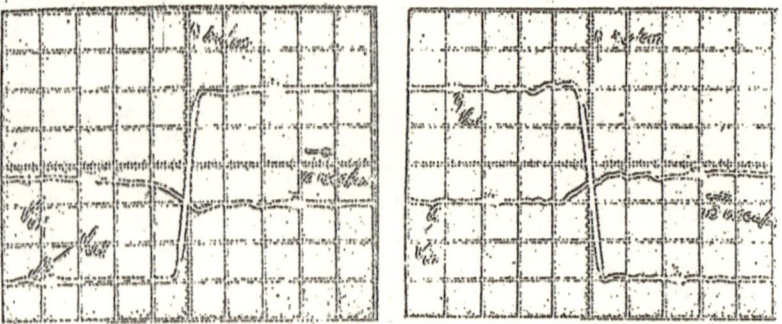

Figure 6
DRIVER CIRCUIT
and its transient performance
with ≈20 pF loading on output.

b. Sense Circuit

Figure 7 is a schematic of the digit driver and the interface to the sense amplifier.

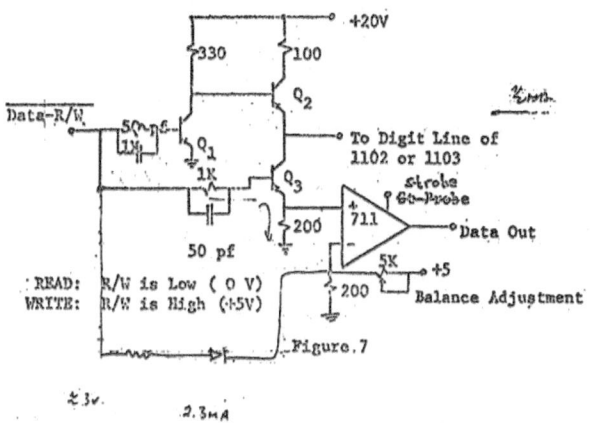

Figure 7

READ: R/W is Low (0 V)
WRITE: R/W is High (+5V)

For writing into the memory R/W is high. If data is high, then the input to the digit driver is low. Thus, Q_1 and Q_3 are turned off and Q_2 is turned on. This pulls the digit input to the memory up to +20V (logic "0"). If data is low, then the input is high. In this case, Q_1 and Q_3 are on and Q_2 is off. The digit line is then pulled down to ground potential through the on resistance of Q_3 in series with the 200Ω resistor (logic "1").

For writing into the memory R/W is high. ... ...
the input to the digit driver is low. Thus, Q_1 and Q_3 are turned off and Q_2 is turned on. This pulls the digit input to the memory up to +20V (logic "0"). If data is low, then the input is high. In this case, Q_1 and Q_3 are on and Q_2 is off. The digit line is then pulled down to ground potential through the on resistance of Q_3 in series with the 200Ω resistor (logic "1").

- 11 -

b. Sense Circuit (continued)

For read, R/W is low, so the input to the digit driver is high. The digit line is returned to ground independently of the state of the data input. If a "0" had been stored in the memory approximately 300 μA would flow out of the digit line and produce 60 mv of signal across the 200Ω resistor. This would produce 5V pulse at the output of the μA 711 amplifier. If a "1" had been stored in the memory, no current flows and the amplifier output would remain at ~0 V.

1102 - 1024-Bit Dynamic RAM
(Rev. 2, 5/14/70)

DESCRIPTION

The 1102 is a fully decoded random access memory in a 1024 x 1 bit organization in a lea' hermetic DIP package. This circuit is intended for applications where cost is of pr importance and moderate performance (345 ns access time) is acceptable. The device requi 20V clock and address amplitudes. Separate input/output lines are provided.

CHARACTERISTICS

Mode of operation	Clocked NDRO
Temp range	0 to 70°C
Access time*	345 ns
Cycle time	500 ns
Refresh rate**	2 ms over temperature
V_{SS}	+20V ± 1V
V_{BB}	V_{SS} + 2.0V
V_{DD}	0V
All inputs "HIGH"	V_{SS} +.3 / -1.0V
"LOW"	0V ± 1.0V
Output current	≥ 333 μA
Output voltage	≥ 60 mV (R_L = 180Ω)
Capacitance:	
Address lines	7 pf
Digit line	5 pf
PRECH	25 pf
YENBL	10 pf
CENBL	10 pf
Power dissipation:	
Peak	500 μW/bit
Average	125 μW/bit
Standby	50 μW/bit

PIN CONFIGURATION

BLOCK DIAG.

TIMING DIAGRAM

COMMENTS

* Clock rise and fall times are ≤ 20 ns.
** All X addresses must be cycled (?/6 clock cycles) to completely refresh the memory.

Every 2 msec
150 pf. load prose.

1102, 1103 Sense a ps

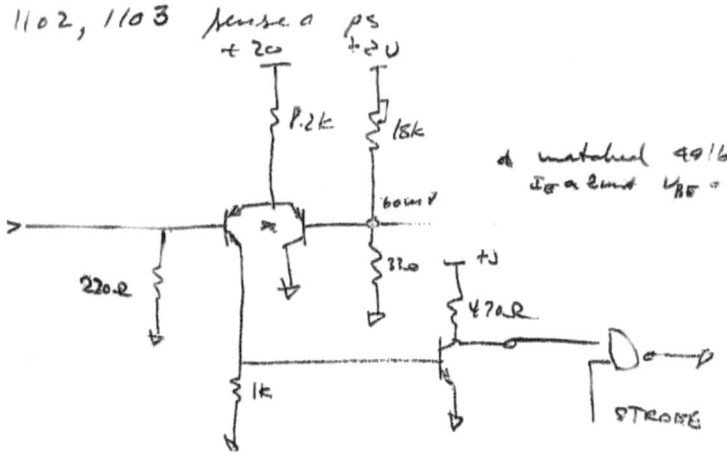

Cheap sense amp.

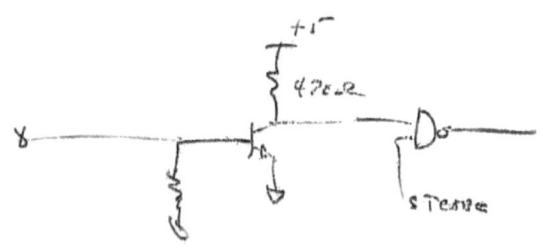

1102 = 330 µA
1103 = ≥ 1 mA
1104 = ≥ 2 mA

9/10/70

 INTEL CORPORATION 365 Middlefield Road, Mountain View, California 94040 • (415) 969-1670

PRELIMINARY DATA SHEET

1103

1024-bit Dynamic Random Access Memory

DEVICE OPERATION:

Device operation can be understood via the block diagram, Figure 1, and the timing diagram, Figure 2. An access cycle begins T_{AC} time before the negative transition of CENBL. During this period, PRECH is active, and the row and column decoders settle to their chosen states. Next, during the period T_{OV}, the contents of the 32 cells along the selected row are written into the 32 refresh amplifiers, one of which is required for each column in the array. During this overlap interval, the R DATA output is unconditionally held HIGH by the selected column amplifier. At the positive transition of PRECH, the contents of the refresh amplifiers are written back into their respective columns, and the R DATA output validly depicts the state of the selected cell T_{PO} later. A suitable time T_{PW} after the positive edge of PRECH, the state of the W DATA line may be copied into the selected cell, using a WRITE pulse of minimum duration T_W.

The device exhibits three characteristics of considerable importance in system design:

1) The memory cells are dynamic in nature, and thus require periodic data refreshing. This is accomplished by selecting the chip, (pulsing its clocks) and cycling through the 32 states of the A_1 through A_5 inputs. This operation must be performed no less often than every 2 milliseconds.

2) The device dissipates maximum power while the PRECH input is negative; as this input runs 40% duty cycle, at minimum cycle time, dissipation is typically 250 mW in normal operation. If, however, PRECH were to remain LOW in anticipation of an access, standby power would soar to over 500 mW. It is thus necessary to relax PRECH to its positive state between accesses.

3) Cell readout is nondestructive; the read/write cycle depicted in the timing diagram may be shortened for a read only or refresh only cycle, as the WRITE pulse is only required for entry of new data. Thus a read only or refresh only cycle can be T_W shorter than a Read/Write cycle, or a Write only cycle.

Project RAM 1102/1103 1024 bit

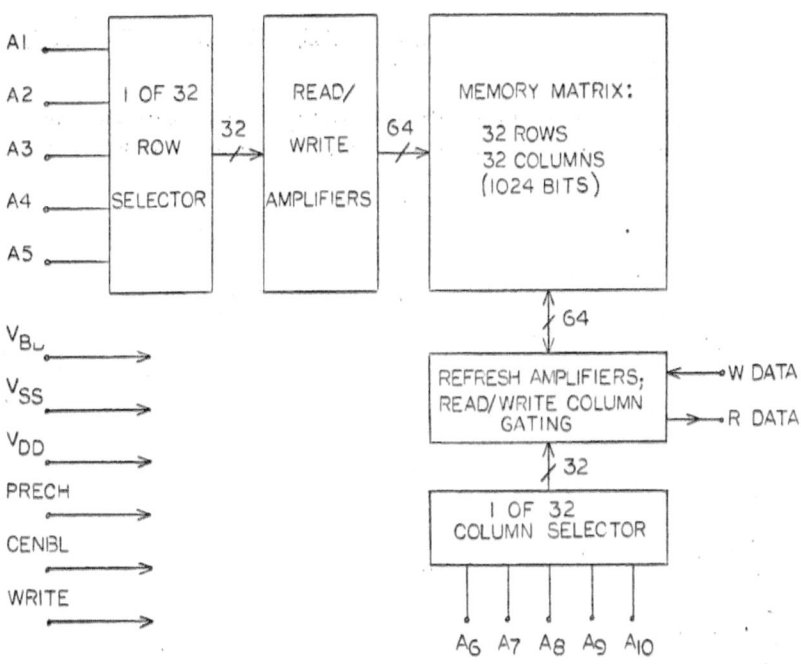

FIGURE 1: BLOCK DIAGRAM 1103

The 1102s were in a 16 pin package using the package top for a 17th connection to provide the needed bias for the device to function. Intel put 1103 in an 18 pin package for this reason.

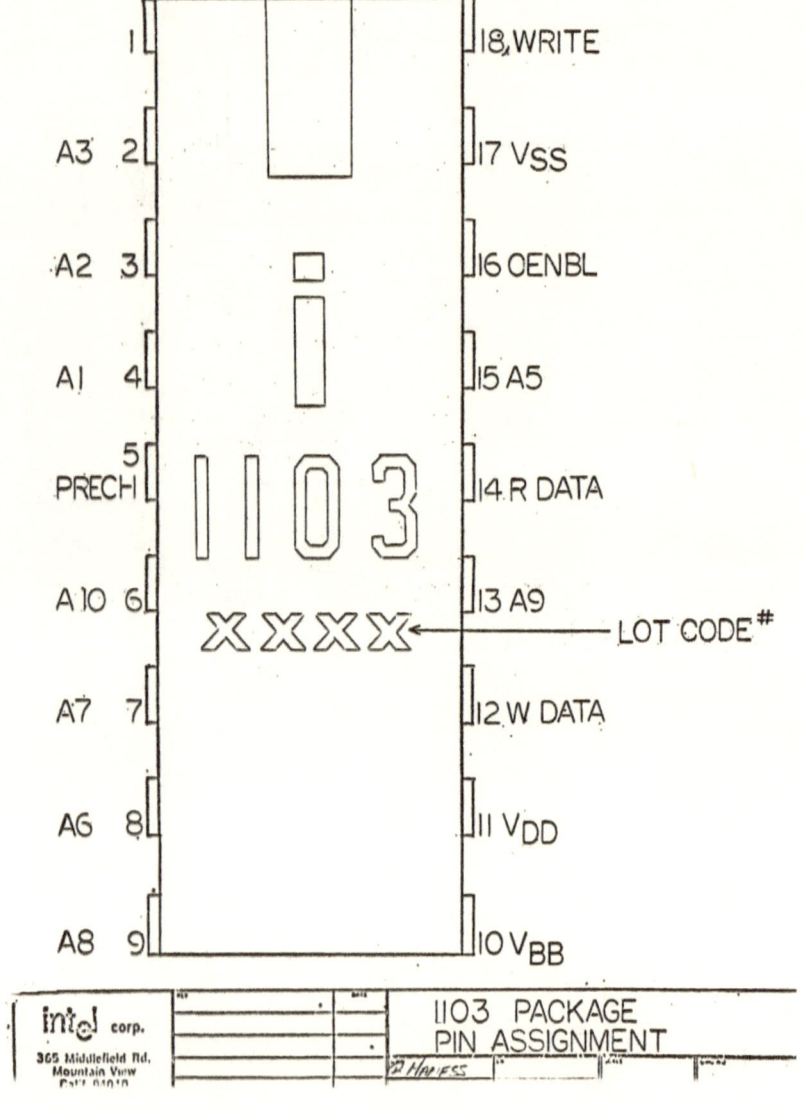

Project RAM 1102/1103 1024 bit

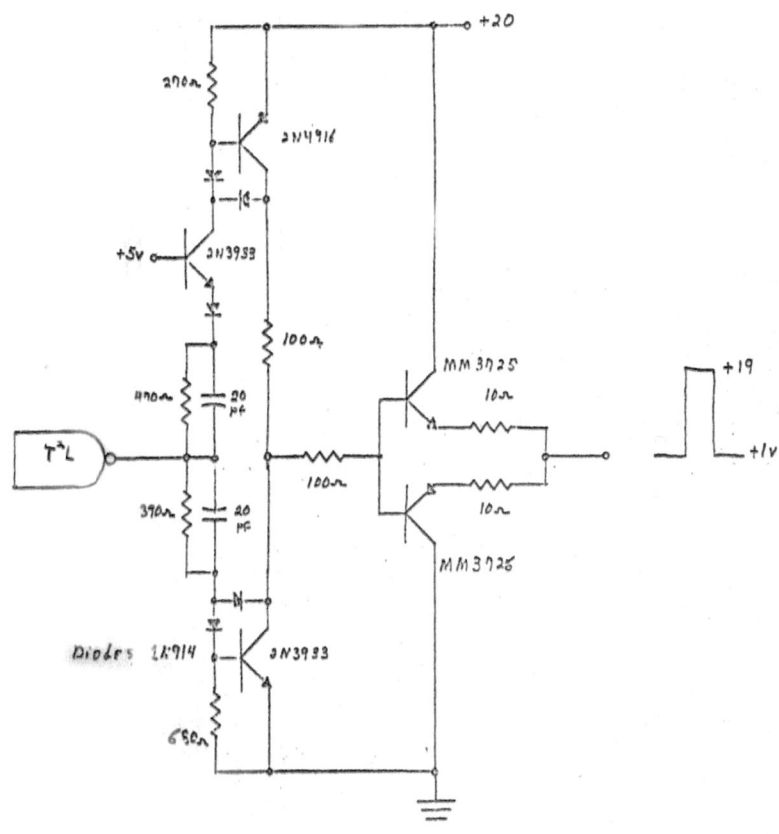

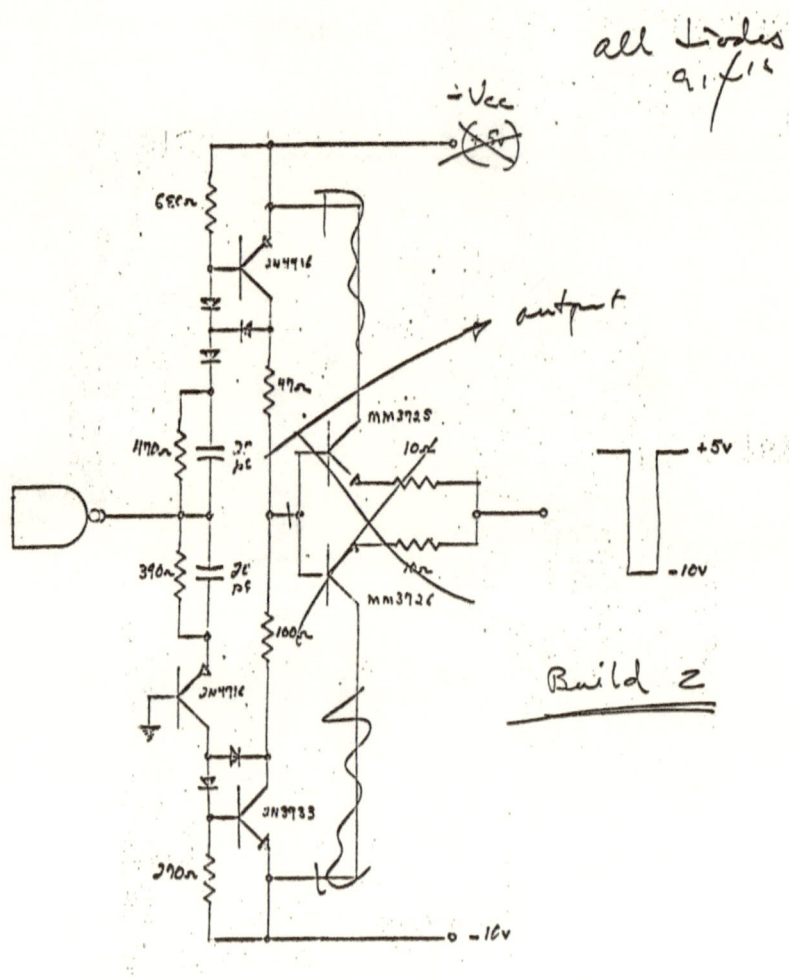

Project RAM 1102/1103 1024 bit

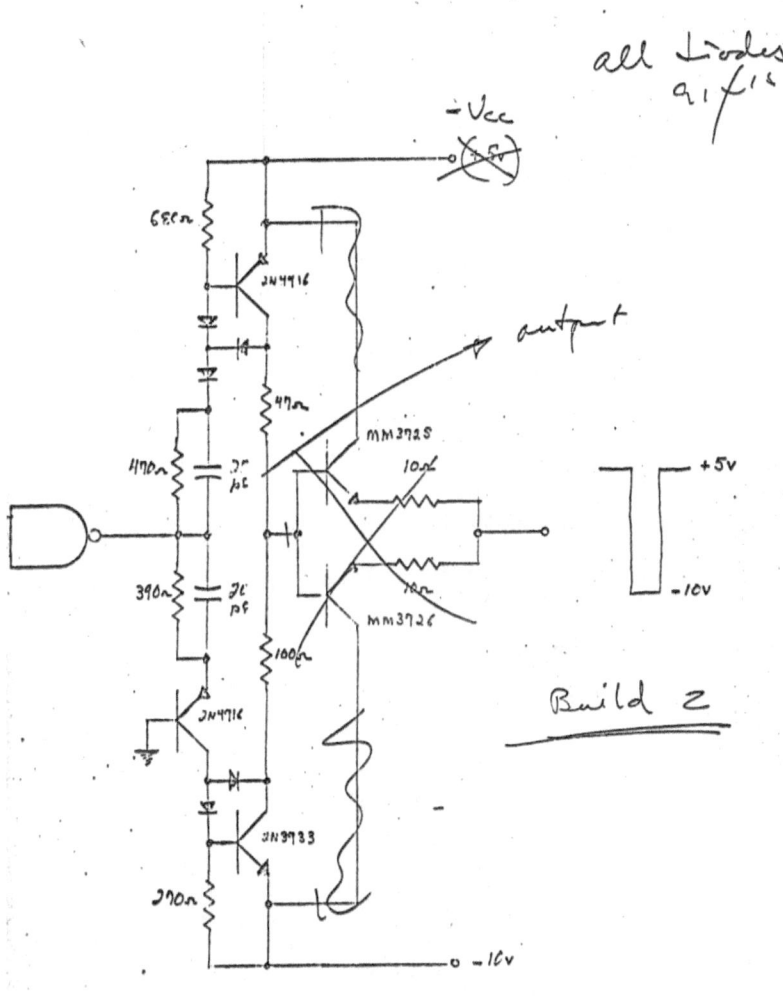

MOS LSI Memory 1103

INTEL CORP. 365 Middlefield Road, Mountain View, California 94040 • (415) 969-1670

JANUARY 1971

FULLY DECODED RANDOM ACCESS 1024 BIT DYNAMIC MEMORY

- Low Power Dissipation — Dissipates Power Primarily on Selected Chips
- Access Time — 300 nsec
- Cycle Time — 580 nsec
- Refresh Period...Every 2 milliseconds for 0–70° C
- OR-Tie Capability
- Simple Memory Expansion — Chip Enable Input Lead
- Fully Decoded — on Chip Address Decode
- Inputs Protected — All Inputs Have Protection Against Static Charge
- Low Cost Packaging — 18 Pin Plastic Dual In-Line Configuration

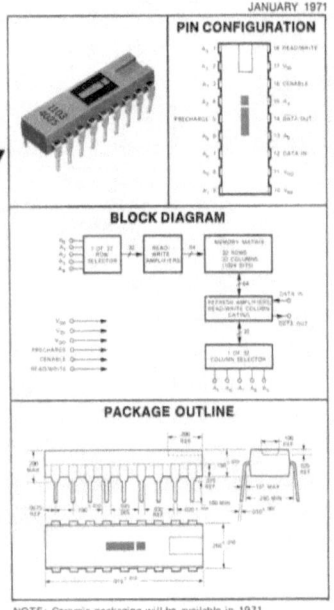

NOTE: Ceramic packaging will be available in 1971

The Intel 1103 is designed primarily for main memory applications where high performance, low cost, and large bit storage are important design objectives.

It is a 1024 word by 1 bit random access memory element using normally off P-channel MOS devices integrated on a monolithic array. It is fully decoded, permitting the use of an 18 pin dual in-line package. It uses dynamic circuitry and primarily dissipates power only during precharge.

Information stored in the memory is non-destructively read. Refreshing of all 1024 bits is accomplished in 32 read cycles and is required every two milliseconds.

A separate **cenable** (chip enable) lead allows easy selection of an individual package when outputs are OR-tied.

The Intel 1103 is fabricated with **silicon gate technology**. This **low threshold** technology allows the design and production of higher performance MOS circuits and provides a higher functional density on a monolithic chip than conventional MOS technologies.

Intel's silicon gate technology also provides excellent protection against contamination. This permits the use of low cost plastic packaging.

Copyright Intel Corporation 1971. Contents may not be reproduced in whole or part without the written consent of Intel Corporation.

1970. Other Intel Data Sheets

Bipolar LSI Memory **3101**

INTEL CORP. 365 Middlefield Road. Mountain View, California 94040 • (415) 969-1670

HIGH SPEED FULLY DECODED 64 BIT MEMORY

- Fast Access Time -- 60 nsec.
- Low Power Dissipation -- 6 mW/bit
- DTL and TTL Compatible -- Inputs are One TTL Load. Outputs Sink 20 mA.
- OR-Tie Capability.
- Simple Memory Expansion -- Chip Select Input Lead.
- Fully Decoded -- on Chip Address Decode and Buffer.
- Minimum Line Reflection -- Low Voltage Diode Input Clamp.
- Standard Packaging -- 16 Pin Dual In-Line Lead Configuration.

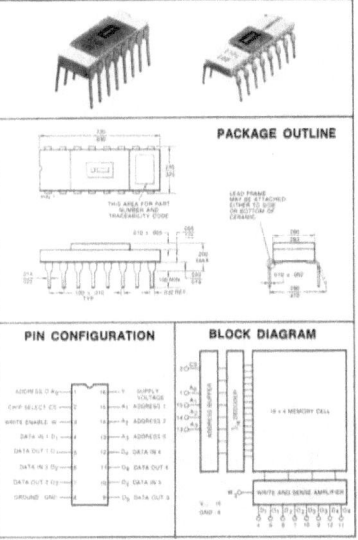

The Intel 3101 is a 64 bit random access memory. Its high speed makes it ideal in scratch pad applications.

The use of Schottky barrier diode clamped transistors to obtain fast switching speeds results in higher performance than equivalent devices made with a gold diffusion process.

The Intel 3101 is packaged in a hermetically sealed 16 pin dual in-line package, and its performance is specified over a temperature range from 0° - 85°C.

This device is organized as a 16 word by 4 bit array.

The storage flip-flops are addressed through an on chip 1 of 16 binary decoder using four input address leads.

A separate Chip Select lead allows easy selection of an individual package when outputs are OR tied.

In addition to the address leads and the Chip Select lead, there is a write input which allows data presented at the data leads to be entered at the addressed storage cells.

MOS LSI Memory **1101, 11011**

INTEL CORP. 365 Middlefield Road, Mountain View, California 94040 • (415) 969-1670

FULLY DECODED RANDOM ACCESS 256 BIT MEMORY

- Low Power Dissipation--2 mW/bit During Access--Can Retain Information on Standby at 50 μwatts/bit
- Access Time--Typically Below 1 μsec
- DTL and TTL Compatible--Outputs Drive 2 TTL Loads
- OR-Tie Capability
- Simple Memory Expansion--Chip Select Input Lead
- Fully Decoded--on Chip Address Decode and Sense
- Inputs Protected--All Inputs Have Protection Against Static Charge
- Standard Packaging--16 Pin Dual In-Line Configuration

PACKAGE OUTLINE

PIN CONFIGURATION

BLOCK DIAGRAM

The Intel 1101 is a 256 words by 1 bit random access memory element using normally off P-channel MOS devices integrated on a monolithic array. It is fully decoded, permitting the use of a 16 pin hermetic dual in-line package. It uses fully dc stable (static) circuitry and therefore requires no clocks to operate.

The 1101 will directly interface with standard bipolar integrated logic circuits (TTL, DTL, etc.) There is no need for either special driver circuits or special level converters for inputs or outputs. The data output buffers are capable of driving at least two TTL loads **directly**.

A separate Chip Select lead allows easy selection of an individual package when outputs are OR-tied.

The Intel 1101 is fabricated with **silicon gate technology.** This **low threshold** technology allows the design and production of higher performance MOS circuits and provides a higher functional density on a monolithic chip than conventional MOS technologies.

The 1101 is designed primarily for small buffer store applications where high performance, low cost, and ease of interfacing with other standard logic circuits are important design objectives.

For applications requiring a faster access time we recommend the 11011 which is a selection from the 1101 and has a guaranteed maximum access time of 1 μsec.

 Bipolar ROM Memory **3301, 33011**

INTEL CORP. 365 Middlefield Road, Mountain View, California 94040 • (415) 969-1670

HIGH SPEED FULLY DECODED 1024 BIT READ-ONLY MEMORY

- Fast Access Time -- 60 nsec.
- Low Power Dissipation -- 0.5 mW/bit typical.
- DTL and TTL Compatible -- Input Loading is .25 mA -- Outputs sink 15 mA.
- OR-Tie Capability.
- Simple Memory Expansion -- 2 Chip Select Input Leads.
- Fully Decoded -- on Chip Address Decode and Buffer.
- Minimum Line Reflection -- Low Voltage Diode Input Clamp.
- Standard Packaging -- 16 Pin Dual In-Line Lead Configuration.

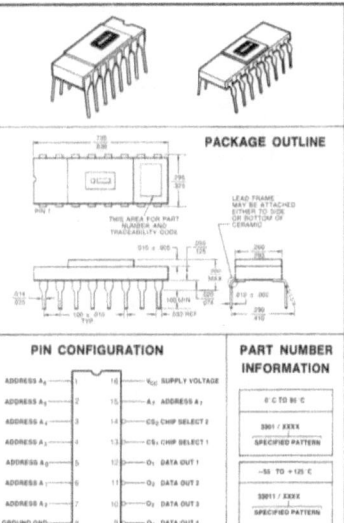

The Intel 3301 family is a 1024 bit read-only memory. Its high speed makes it ideal in microprogram and table lookup applications.

The use of Schottky barrier diode clamped transistors to obtain fast switching speeds results in higher performance than equivalent devices made with a gold diffusion process. The Intel 3301 is packaged in a hermetically sealed 16 pin dual in-line package, and its performance is specified over temperature ranges of 0° - 85°C (3301) and −55°C to +125°C (33011).

These devices are organized as 256 word by 4 bit arrays.

Storage bits are addressed through an on chip 1 of 256 binary decoder using 8 input address leads.

Two separate Chip Select leads allow easy selection of an individual package when outputs are OR tied. Expansion to 2048 words can be done with the addition of only 2 quad gates.

The 3301 family is offered in **standard** "off the shelf" configurations as well as in special configurations designed for your **Customized** needs. The **Applications** section of this data sheet describes both types.

MOS LSI Shift Register **1406, 1506, 1407, 1507**

INTEL CORP. 365 Middlefield Road, Mountain View, California 94040 · (415) 969-1670

DUAL 100 BIT DYNAMIC SHIFT REGISTER

- Low Power Dissipation--.4 mW/bit at 1 MHz
- High Frequency Operation -- 2 MHz Guaranteed
- DTL, TTL Compatible
- Low Clock Capacitance -- 40 pF
- Low Clock Leakage -- ≤.5 µA at −18 V
- Inputs Protected Against Static Charge
- Standard Packaging -- Low Profile TO-5
- Military and Commercial Temperature Ranges
- Low Output Impedance -- 300 Ω Typical

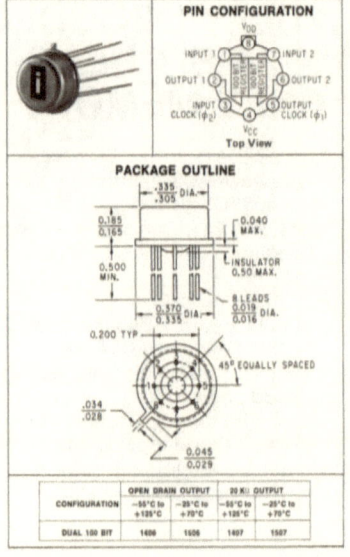

The Intel dual 100 bit dynamic shift register element consists of normally off P-channel MOS devices integrated on a monolithic array. It uses low voltage circuitry to minimize power dissipation and to facilitate interfacing with bipolar integrated circuits. It uses two clock phases only.

The dual 100 bit device can be driven directly by standard bipolar integrated circuits (TTL, DTL, etc.) or by MOS circuits. The design of the output stage provides driving capability for MOS or bipolar IC's.

Use of the low threshold **silicon gate technology** allows high speed (2 MHz guaranteed), while reducing power dissipation by a factor of 2 and reducing clock input capacitance by a factor of 3 compared to equivalent products manufactured by conventional MOS technologies.

This family is designed for low cost buffer applications. It is available in both military (−55°C to +125°C) and industrial (−25°C to +70°C) grade. It is also available with or without an internal 20K pull-up resistor which may provide easier interfacing to other circuitry.

1970. Other Intel Data Sheets

Bipolar LSI Memory 3102, 3202

INTEL CORP. 365 Middlefield Road, Mountain View, California 94040 • (415) 969-1670

DEC. 1970

PARTIALLY DECODED RANDOM ACCESS 256 BIT BIPOLAR MEMORY (3102) AND BINARY DECODER-DRIVER (3202)

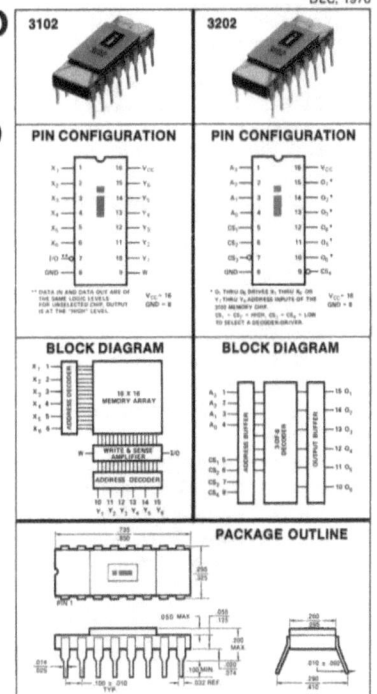

- Fast Access Time—120 ns total— including Decoder-Driver and memory
- Low Memory Power Dissipation— 2.5 mw/bit
- Directly Compatible with DTL and TTL Logic circuits
- OR-tie capability
- Easy Memory Expansion through 4 chip select inputs on Decoder-Driver
- Minimum Line Reflection—low voltage diode input clamp
- Decoder-Driver (3202) Drives at least 32 memory elements, Memory (3102) Output Sinks 15 mA
- Low Input Load Current—.25 mA max., 1/6 Standard TTL Input Load
- Standard Packaging—Decoder and Memory both in 16-pin Dual-In-Line Configuration

The Intel 3102 is a high speed 256-bit bipolar random access Memory, organized as 256 words by 1 bit. The address of the Memory is coded with a special 3-of-6 code which offers low power dissipation and high speed operation for the Memory chip.

The Applications section of this data sheet describes the special 3-of-6 code.

The Intel 3202 is a binary to 3-of-6 decoder-driver, capable of driving thirty-two 3102 Memory Chips. The use of 4 chip select inputs provides expansion of up to 4096 words without additional decoding.

Both the 3102 and 3202 are packaged in hermetically sealed 16 pin dual-in-line packages, and their performance is specified over the temperature range of 0°–85°C. The use of Schottky barrier diode clamped transistors to obtain fast switching speeds results in higher performance than equivalent devices made with a gold diffusion process.

 MOS LSI Shift Registers **1402, 1403, 1404**

INTEL CORP. 365 Middlefield Road, Mountain View, California 94040 • (415) 969-1670

JANUARY 1971

1024 BIT DYNAMIC SHIFT REGISTER

- Low Power Dissipation--.1 mW/bit at 1 MHz
- High Frequency Operation-- 5 MHz Guaranteed
- Low Frequency Operation-- 400 Hz at 25°C Guaranteed
- DTL, TTL Compatible
- Low Clock Capacitance--140 pF
- Low Clock Leakage-- ≤1 uA at −17 V
- Inputs Protected Against Static Charge
- Standard Packaging--8 Lead Low Profile TO-5, 16 Pin Dual In-Line
- Three Standard Configurations -- Quad 256 Bit--1402, Dual 512 Bit--1403, Single 1024 Bit--1404

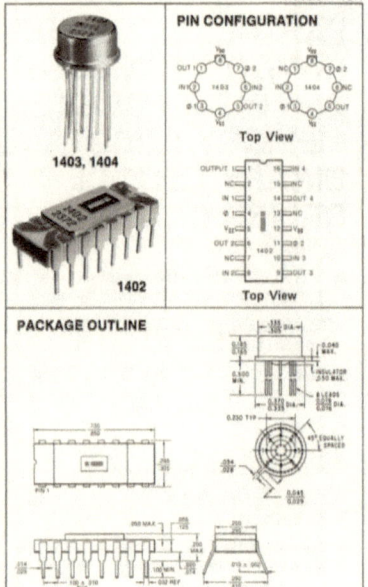

The Intel 1024 Bit dynamic shift register consists of normally off P-channel MOS devices integrated on a monolithic chip. The use of low voltage circuitry minimizes power dissipation and facilitates interfacing with bipolar integrated circuits.

These registers can be driven directly by standard bipolar integrated circuits (TTL, DTL, etc.) or by MOS circuits. The design of the output stage provides driving capability for both MOS and bipolar IC's.

Use of low threshold **silicon gate technology** allows high speed (5 MHz guaranteed) while reducing power dissipation by a factor of **two** and clock input capacitance by a factor of **three** compared to equivalent products manufactured by conventional technologies.

The 1402/3/4 family is designed for low cost memory and delay line applications. Due to "on chip" multiplexing the data rate is twice the clock rate. Data is shifted one bit on each clock pulse (both ϕ_1 and ϕ_2).

Copyright Intel Corporation 1971. Contents may not be reproduced in whole or part without the written consent of Intel Corporation.

1971. My two marriages: Eva and Intel

The title may seem peculiar, but I have not found a better way to define the year in which two completely different realities fell on me.

One of her most common comments from Eva at the time was: "I do not know if you think more about me or if you think more about Intel!"

Undoubtedly 1971 was the most complex year of my life, for personal and business reasons.

It was at the beginning of that year that Eva and I decided to get married and at the same time, I took the decision to go ahead with my small company, still in incubation and not pursuing other activities.

When graduated engineers were in short supply. I received job offers from several large Italian companies like Enel and others well known in the industry. Even Noyce, during his Italian tour, offered me an opportunity to be part of, the just born, Intel company.

More, Eva and I had to decide the date of our marriage, not easy for me due to the many commitments I had personally to carry on.

Eva proposed insistently May or June, but how could I take a honeymoon and get away from all those commitments that were requiring my daily presence?

I was inclined to defer the date as much as possible, looking for a quieter period.

In short, in the end, I managed to convince Eva that the best time for both would have been August, the month when in Italy all business practically shut down for the yearly vacation.

One can imagine the reaction of our parents, relatives, and friends when we officially announced our marriage for Tuesday, August 10, 1971, when in Italy everybody is on vacation. But it was the best solution for me.

I didn't specify to Eva my whole plan that was including a visit to Intel at Santa Clara during our honeymoon: two birds with one stone!

Anyhow, I left for Eva to decide where to marry and she decided on the oldest Milan Church Sant'Ambrogio. There were just a few friends and relatives that could afford to be present.

The next day we flew to San Francisco where we stayed at the Royal Coach Inn in San Mateo, kindly booked for us by Intel.

11 Agosto 1971. San Mateo, Royal Coach Inn

We spent a few days in the area and I visited Intel alone at the new Intel building in Santa Clara on Bower Avenue where I again met with Bob Noyce, Gordon Moore, and Mike Markkula.

This new, modern and still incomplete factory impressed me a lot. I wondered how the just born Intel could grow so quickly

1971. My two marriages: Intel and Eva

and be crowded with staff, including the Italian Federico Faggin, whom I met there for the first time.

August 1971 – The new Intel factory at Santa Clara

Jens Paulsen was there too, and his assistance was very helpful to me, while my angry wife was waiting for my return to the hotel!

August 1971 - With Jens Paulsen, European Marketing Director

This second visit confirmed how right I had been by choosing to become part of Intel.

But now, I had to save my marriage from the furious reaction of Eve, abandoned in the hotel, since I had not informed her about my plans to visit Intel.

After various meetings with Noyce, Moore, Graham, Markkula, Ted Hoff, and others, I collected documentation and notes useful for my activity when returned to Italy, and then I drove back to San Mateo.

At the hotel, the sweet and sulky Eva was waiting for me to move to our next destination, the Holiday Inn in Monterey, booked by Intel and recognized as a famous destination for honeymooners, but my problems with Eva didn't end there!

We were in one of the best-known places for the Americans an area for rich Californians, a destination known for quiet and luxurious honeymoons. But, despite this fame, I must say that this place for us Italians was a real negative surprise.

It was the second half of August and instead of being in front of a beach with a warm sea, as we were used in Italy, it was a cold fog and on the beautiful and spacious beach in front of the hotel, we could not even walk without winter-style clothing.

Not to mention the ocean water, cold as ice, and on which a cold wind was blowing. We felt like we were in Norway and not in a warm Californian area.

To us, inexperienced, it was then explained that the polar cold current from the north was the reason for such a temperature. But for us, a couple of Italians used to sunbath in the Mediterranean sun it was a tragic surprise: our honeymoon was almost ruined.

Eva, who had finally discovered this trip to be in a kind of business trip and, more, at such kind of cold weather was reproaching me saying phrases like: "here is you and your Intel, if we went to Sicily instead, the sea would have been much warmer and we could swim, etc. etc.". I certainly could not blame her!

August 1971, Monterey, Holiday Inn ... on an almost winter day

I was between two fires; I did not know much about America, nor where to move, but I had to agree that she was right.

We could not spend most of our honeymoon in the fog, dressed as in winter and without being able to touch the ocean.

I was getting desperate and I decided to call Jean Noyce's secretary to ask for any help.

I must say that she immediately understood my situation and suggested a fantastic solution, she said: "Why don't you fly to Hawaii, that's an ideal place for a honeymoon and you will find much warmer weather there!"

My answer was of the kind: "And how can I get there and who knows how much it might cost to me!".

She replied to not be afraid, she would ask her travel agent and would call me back in due time.

As a test of American efficiency, she called back in less than half an hour and told me that there was a flight from San Francisco the next day and I could jump on board if booked immediately. And I could get a package including two weeks at the Hotel Maui Lu Resort in Maui.

Furthermore, she confirmed that we could get an all-inclusive offer, flights + hotel at a cost that would be lower than the two weeks at Monterey.

In just a second, I confirmed over the phone. The next morning, we boarded from San Francisco to Honolulu and then to the island of Maui and the Resort where we found a dream place on a warm beach by a calm ocean.

Trips to Hawaii at that time were particularly encouraged with ultra-discounted tour packages; much different from today since Hawaii has become a destination of unrestrained tourism.

I must say that luck, via Intel, assisted me and my honeymoon. While it started not so well, it ended wonderfully.

Moreover, when we arrived at the resort in Maui we found a beautiful floral arrangement with a greeting card signed by Bob Noyce and Mike Markkula.

Agosto 1971. Flowers sent by Noyce and Markkula

We wholeheartedly thank the authors for such a kind gesture that was a great surprise and showed to Eva how Intel people were sensitive. She began to understand that what was going on was more than a simple business relationship.

Eva finally understood why I appreciated Intel, not just for the economic objectives, but certainly for their exquisite attention.

Maui proved to be a beautiful island, almost deserted, with a wonderful temperature, and we would never have imagined such a paradise for our honeymoon thanks to a fantastic Intel secretary who saved our honeymoon.

Agosto 1971 - Maui Lu Resort, Maui, Hawaii

We spent those two weeks driving around the isle, even driving through a normally "off-limits" area reserved to native people, climbing to the top of an extinct volcano, Haleakala, reachable only by driving over a bumpy road at over 3,000 meters of altitude.

The breathtaking view

After our unforgettable stay in Hawaii, we left Honolulu for San Francisco and then Boston for a short stay and finally then back to Italy.

The year 1971 was a period of great growth both for my family and my business: the sale of Intel products picked up and Eva in November announced me we were expecting a baby; our first children Emanuele arrived on July 10, 1972.

I had increased the staff at my small office in Milan and many companies have been ordering Intel samples.

Visits from Intel continued and we were now able to carry out business negotiations for Intel products by ourselves.

Robert Noyce visited Italy a second time and we went together to Olivetti to meet Prof. Pier Giorgio Perotto, head of the research and development division. We discussed the use of semiconductor memories in many projects.

During the same meeting Ing. Rivara, head of the design department showed an interest in using both 256-bit i1101 and the 1024-bit i1103 memory devices.

Soon Camillo Vitale joined my company from Siemens and he was helping Jens Paulsen in organizing a tour to potential Italian clients.

1971. My two marriages: Intel and Eva

Ime, Selenia, Contraves, Litton, GTE, Lagomarsino, Fiat, Pignone, and at least 20 other main industrial companies became clients for Intel memory products.

Ted Hoff came to Italy in December of 1971 and I visited Olivetti with him where we had a very interesting business day talking to many managers there.

Hoff, on top of his memories, mentioned the new 4-bit CPU project that Ted Hoff was carrying on while Dr. Rivara confirmed his interest in the new 1024-bit N-Channel i2102 memory. Later, Olivetti qualified this memory and purchased it in very large quantities.

Dr. Dalmasso was looking for a custom chip integrating an entire desktop computer which, he said, should cost in large quantities no more than 25 $.

Dalmasso discussed some of his confidential projects, a desktop calculator with a 13-digit display. A second project of which I took note, was a portable CMOS calculator powered by a single 1.5-volt battery. He thought that it could be produced in very large quantities making it interesting to Intel.

Finally, we talked about a desktop calculator with 12 or 16 digit liquid crystal display to be launched starting in the year 1973.

Ted Hoff returned to California convinced of the importance of Italy and Olivetti for the Intel market and the need to pursue any possible "design-in" opportunities there.

A new and equally stimulating period awaited me for the years to come and, besides the business, I had to care also of my growing family.

Our first child would be followed by three more. My family seemed to grow almost at the same speed as Intel.

I remember the many nice lunches with Intel people around Ivrea, the Olivetti location, often drinking the best local wines. But, being the driver, I had to limit myself. Not so my kind American guests!

As a corporate gift, I began to procure rare bottles of wine and offer them to Intel visitors who seemed to like these wines very much, well beyond my expectations.

Particular lovers of those wines were Tom Lawrence and Bob Noyce. As a proof, I still keep the following card that Mrs. Ann Bowers and Bob Noyce sent to me after I insisted that Bob board the plane returning to the US with a box of Carema red wine. I do not know how he managed to pass the American customs controls, but the card below shows that he succeeded.

December 1977. Thank you card from Ann and Bob Noyce

Following years with Intel

It was the year 1973 when the interaction between Intel and the Olivetti design group headed by prof. Pier Giorgio Perotto was intensified. There were continuous meetings in Ivrea and I kept numerous notes including the names of the various characters involved.

Among those names I have being dealing I should mention here Salvini, Conca, Lepri, Maero, Sacchetto, Franti, Santerini, Fumagalli, Fogaroli, De Monte, Fiorenza, Priest, Ferroglio, De Sandre, Mercurio, Vittorelli, Giordani, Lanza, Rivara all of them engaged in projects involving Intel products.

At the end of that year, an opportunity occurred that showed how the system designers at Olivetti were at that time more advanced than those in Santa Clara. The 8008 microprocessor needed an urgent series of peripheral chips to be useful at the client site.

It was decided that to help Intel it would be necessary to send an Olivetti designer from Ivrea to Santa Clara to work with Intel engineers and help them to implement those peripherals.

Lucio Lanza, a young engineer at Olivetti was chosen for this mission by prof. Perotto. I knew Lanza well through visiting Olivetti and I backed up this idea, hoping that it would strengthen the ties between Intel and Olivetti, my largest client in Italy.

I met Lanza at my house in Milan before his trip to the US for his future mission and I kept myself in touch with him and we met in California a few times during my visits to Intel.

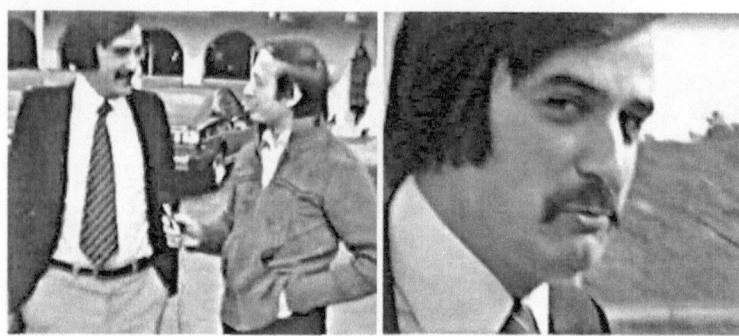
1977 – Palo Alto, Lucio Lanza speaking at an interview

Lanza, thanks to his experience, was able to design in a short time three devices that were quickly implemented in silicon: the CRT controller, the disk controller, and the DMA controller.

Unfortunately, when he finished his work, Lanza did not return to Italy and was hired by Intel as a design engineer. The matter did not please in Olivetti and I had some trouble calming Perotto who was very angry at Intel for that hiring him.

I can't forget a meeting held by Intel at St. Moritz in Switzerland where all European distributors met December 1975 celebrating the sales results achieved in Europe.

Noyce was a great skier, he defeated all the participants on the ski slopes and particularly he defeated me, a very poor skier.

Tom Lawrence, head of Europe, another great skier, was the only one able to compete with Noyce.

I confess that I feared for their integrity and, consequently, for the Intel business since those two managers were an essential part of the company.

On that occasion, I took photos of the events, and now I can offer them to readers

Looking at my pictures it might seem that those meetings were just a kind of entertainment, but it was not so. Intel was great and generous, but we were working all day long.

Each European distributor had to present in front of the American and European managers a series of slides containing very detailed market data by product, by customer, and by region and they had to answer the many questions coming from each Intel product manager. This was a very smart way to gather in a few days a, detailed and reliable, market survey on the entire European market!

St. Moritz, Dec 1975 - Robert Noyce speaking at the Intel sales meeting

Each European distributor had to present on the blackboard and in front of the American and European leaders a series of slides, each prepared by Intel marketing.

St. Moritz, Dec 1975 - Tom Lawrence, President Europe

Each slide had to contain a series of sales data by product type and by the customer and each Intel product manager could ask his questions. For each product, we had to show a forecast by the customer and detailed information about our organization.

In a few days, Intel could achieve a detailed picture of their International business and to take those needed actions with full knowledge about the market.

It was a great job of "intelligence", remunerated with a nice stay in pleasant places!

St. Moritz, Dec 1975 - Ed Gelbach (left) and Hal Feeney

Guy Debruyne in the middle with Gert Griese on the right

St. Moritz. At my right Ted Kenny, president of the Israeli distributor

Those meetings were also a great opportunity to meet other distributors and to talk about the difficulties in selling particular products and to exchange information, sometimes even critical, about our Principals.

I remember Nomblot of the French Tekelek, J. Piens of the Belgian Inelco, G. Wolf of the German E. 2000, and J. Rommer of the Norwegian Nordisk Electronik.

The Rise of Intel Business

The solid-state market and the Intel business exploded in the seventies. The cold war, the space race, and the pervasiveness of these products practically dominated every electronic system.

Large computers had discarded vacuum tubes completely and solid-state components became the heart of every new design including cars, missiles, planes, telephones, etc.

Telecommunications and optical fibers became part of very fast networks, light-emitting diodes, (today LEDs), appeared on the market and soon they replaced the helium-neon gas lasers and found applications in many fields.

There was an explosion of new applications comparable to the Cambrian geological era for the biological world; the solid-state technology born in 1948 with a tiny point-contact transistor was now spreading around as none could even imagine.

For the first time in human history, technology will have an exponential development, the effects of which we can verify today, and I was proud to be part of it thanks to Intel.

The foundations for creating Intel, the greatest chip industry of our time, were laid.

In that stormy ocean, I saw myself as being on the deck of a small ship in whose sail the wind of the god Aeolus was blowing, under the guise of Intel.

I did not have just to sell these new components, but following what Ed Gelbach once said: "It's not enough to offer the microprocessors to the market, we have to teach customers how to use them.", and he was right.

And I had to create new structures to offer qualified training courses, dependable documentation and, first I had to create a qualified sales force.

To fulfill these needs, in Italy we created two companies wholly dedicated to educating the market by publishing specialized books and a technical magazine dedicated to design engineers.

Eledra Systems Spa and Edelektron Srl started operating during the early nineties to complement the activity of Eledra 3S.

They operated closely with Intel by exploiting its scientific production and taking advantage of their teachers, like Stan Mazor who personally held microprocessor courses in Italy.

Eledra staff soon needed new managers: Dr. Aldo Meneghelli joined us from Philips and DEC, Dr. Giorgio Grigoletti joined us from Olivetti and my brother Umberto Accenti joined us from the publishing world.

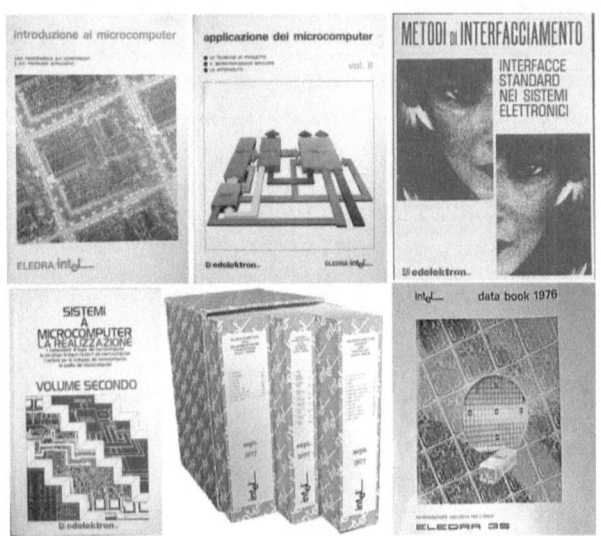

Eledra publications to help designers: a total of 3,000 pages

The Rise of Intel Business

The 3 volumes of blue Intel Data Books shown above was a 1,500 pages collection of the original Intel data sheets and application notes, printed in Italy during the year 1977.

All that effort was an important part of the success of Intel products among the Italian industry.

Milan, 1973. Microprocessor seminar. From right Guy De Bruyne, Stan Mazor, Tom Lawrence and last at left, Gert Griese

Reading my calendars covering that period there are no doubts that the Italian industry understood clearly the importance of the new electronic era and that they were eager to use the new Intel components.

Seminars and courses were announced on our periodical ETN

We didn't miss any important Italian exhibition, the most important of which was BIAS held in Milan.

Eledra 3S. Two images of exhibitions cooperating with Intel

The Rise of Intel Business

Starting in the year 1978 we created a bimonthly magazine called "Eledra Top News" (ETN) containing an updated set of technical information about the products distributed by Eledra.

Soon we added interviews to various Intel managers, in this way their messages reached everywhere in Italy, as the magazine was the most read among the specialized newspapers.

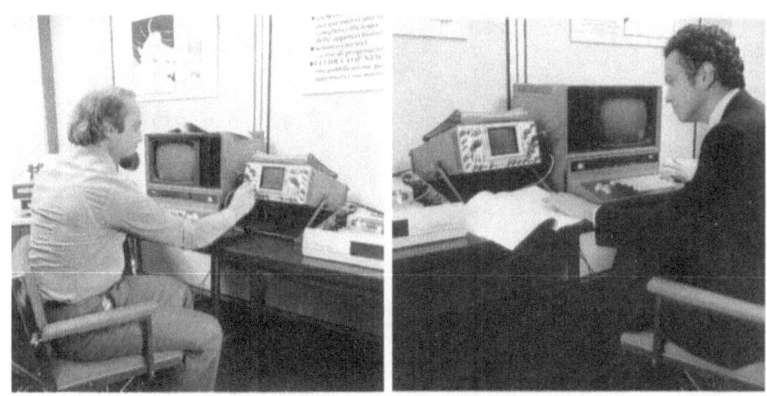

Dr. Grigoletti ed Dr. Meneghelli working at Intellec Development Systems

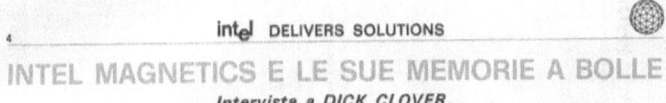

Dick Clover announcing Intel magnetic memories

Hank O'Hara speaks about the market

1978. Andy Grove commenting the market

The Rise of Intel Business

Tom Lawrence commenting the European chip market

1980. Jack Carsten commenting the microprocessor market

With success selling Intel products we became soon the largest organization distributing electronic components in our country and we had to move to a much larger facility in Milan. Relocation and moving were managed by Evart Srl, an interior decorating company founded by my wife Eva in the year 1973.

The quartz watch: An Intel disaster

Intel desperate wanted to diversify into other markets where its chips, produced in large volume could make a difference. To do this the company bought a small start-up called Microma.

Microma has been the first to design a quartz wristwatch with a liquid crystal display and somebody at Intel thought that the huge watch market could be a good choice. Intel could produce the watch chip that Microma could use in their watch.

I remember very well what was going on at Santa Clara on this subject and talks about the dream of putting a chip in each of the millions of wristwatches sold any year in the world.

The memory market was becoming quite crowded. Many of these competitors were eroding the traditional Intel market and to look for diversification was a natural aspiration.

The big question was where to find a market that could absorb a standard chip by the millions and Intel's the conclusion has to enter the wristwatch market.

When Robert Noyce showed me his first quartz watch that he was wearing with its small liquid crystal display and told me that its precision was on the order of a few seconds per year and didn't need to be recharged every day I wanted to wear one to immediately.

No mechanical watch could compete with it: a technological marvel and I was proud to sell it in Italy and I bought a small quantity to start selling it.

The end-user price was about $ 200. When a lady's version was announced, I was eager to give one to my wife.

I discovered then how far I was, and Intel too, from understanding the end-user market.

Eva had been wearing it, unwillingly, sometime just to make me happy and when I insisted that she should leave the so inferior mechanical wristwatch, she told me bluntly that she didn't care about that crazy precision, she wanted to wear something nice and not a bulky and thick object: for that price she preferred a beautiful Swiss watch, no matter what about technical specifications.

In short, she made me aware that a wristwatch, before being a technological instrument to measure the time was, represented an esthetic status symbol. It was jewelry!

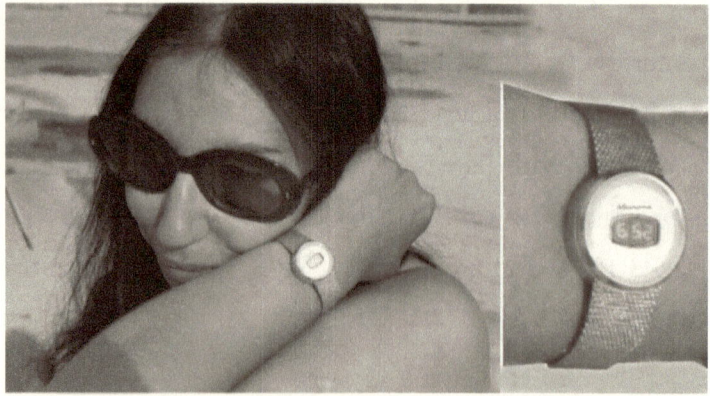

1973. My failing birthday present to my wife

The quartz watch: an Intel disaster

The idea of creating a consumer product with many more features that were acceptable to the public at large would wait another millennium until the Apple Watch. In the meantime, the Japanese would conquer the quartz watch market not for features but through competitive prices.

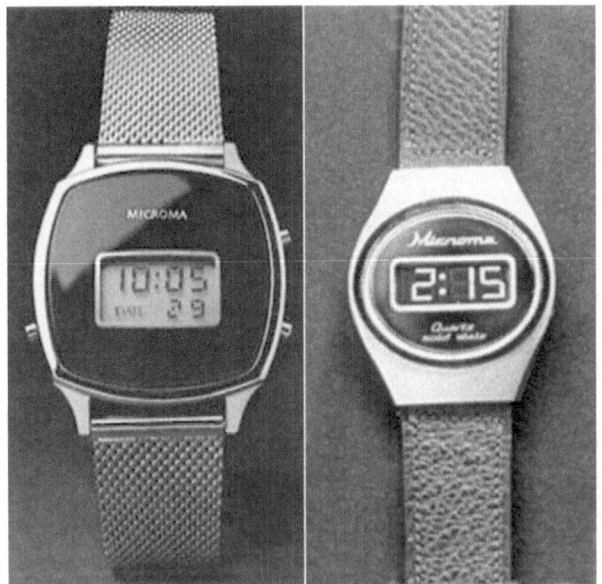

The first and second generation of Microma wristwatches

More importantly, the retail sales channel was foreign to us. Our customers were the industries and to reach the end-user we had to convince the watch dealers to stock and sell our products, an impossible enterprise!

We were an unknown brand with a not so good looking watch and no dealer wanted to show it in their show windows in Milan.

In the end, I barely managed to sell a few watches, at discounted prices almost only to friends and relatives.

A disaster! After that failure, Intel decided to stay away from the consumer market and to manufacture products to be sold to industrial manufacturers who knew well how to sell to the end-users.

A gigantic Olivetti Order

The event that I have reported here date back to the second half of the seventies and concerns about the first 1024-bit static RAM produced by Intel and called i2102.

There was a great technological leap from the previous i1103 which, being of the dynamic type and requiring two voltages to be fed, presented several problems.

The i2102 used only one 5 volts supply and its use was very simple and stable. I immediately presented this new product to Olivetti, and to their qualification laboratory to obtain qualification for their volume production.

There the engineers checked that memory extensively at the end the product got green light toward production.

In the qualification process, many departments have been involved: the purchasing department of the design group, the production department, and finally the department designing the testing systems for checking all components to screen bad units from good ones.

Throughout the process, I had to be very present to overcome any problem arising from their qualification efforts.

When it seemed that everything would be all right, I heard from the production people about a delicate problem that didn't concern Intel itself. That memory was too new on the market and they didn't have the time or the capability to create the software needed by their Sentry testing system to be used in production.

I knew that also Intel was using Sentry systems to test those memories and I thought to that gain a competitive edge I could help Olivetti to solve that problem.

Needless to say, I asked Intel engineers if they could supply that software to Olivetti, but the answer came to me very loudly: "Don't even think we would give out that proprietary software to anybody!".

I could not accept that answer; after all the hard work done to reach that point, I immediately took a flight to San Francisco and went to talk to Jack Carsten about that matter.

He was responsible for world sales and I had a direct and positive relationship with him, more, Jack was also interested in closing that big order.

When I was in Santa Clara he confirmed that to give away the proprietary test software for such an advanced chip would not be an easy problem to solve.

However, he kindly confirmed to me that he would try to get permission from the engineers. He didn't assure me that he could assure success.

I knew that as a world sales manager he was interested to get that gigantic order and he would use his position and power within Intel to help me. So, he told me he would try but suggested me to go back to my hotel and wait there.

I returned to my hotel where my wife Eva was waiting for me. Being November (1975) and having only that commitment, in Italy we had taken the opportunity for a short vacation in California.

A couple of days later Jack called me at the hotel and gave me the happy news that he succeeded in getting permission to

A gigantic Olivetti Order   111

supply the software to Olivetti, provided that they would sign a nondisclosure agreement.

He added that I could now return to Italy and that I could tell Olivetti that Intel would supply the software.

"No way!" I said to Jack, "I'll not move from here without those tapes". To be frank I was afraid that after my departure somebody at Intel could change his mind or that the urgent shipment could be delayed.

So I told Jack: "I'll stay here till when the tapes will be ready", "It may take few days" was jack's answer" and I replied: "Well, no problem, I'll fly to San Diego with Eva and I'll stay there waiting for your call".

I had the feeling that Jack Carsten appreciated my determination and so, while we have been waiting for Jack's call, Eva and myself spent a 5-day unexpected vacation in a magnificent resort in San Diego, at Pacific Oceanfront.

1976 San Diego ... waiting for Jack Carsten's phone call

Finally, the call arrived, we flew to San Francisco and I collected the 20 pounds of tapes that almost filled one of our suitcases. I was hoping not to be checked at the airports smuggling all that material, but everything went OK and I handed over that precious software to Mr. Santerini at Olivetti who signed the Non-Disclosure Agreement.

At that point, the acquisition of the Olivetti order was almost assured.

Even if in the meantime competitors like Texas Instruments and Mostek had been quoting Olivetti for equivalent memories, I was sure that Olivetti would certainly have preferred Intel at similar price conditions, like had been the case.

This sale of the i2102 to Olivetti was regarded as a historic event at Intel and even Bill Davidow wrote a personal dedication about this order in his first book "Marketing High Technology".

As Davidow wisely describes in the above book, selling technology products to the industry is quite a sophisticated job.

It requires that we cover many aspects in dealing with a customer and, on the other hand, the decision-makers at the customer side must evaluate a lot of details of which cost, present, and future, is just one of them.

What I described in this chapter is just one of the many deals I had to manage to reach the goal of getting production orders.

A gigantic Olivetti Order

1986 - Dedication of Bill Davidow in memory of my incredible Olivetti order

This matter was even more complicated with the advent of the microprocessor, the intrinsic importance and value of which were far more significant than simple memories.

We were entering into a new relationship between component suppliers and systems manufacturers.

Almost without realizing it, the CPUs became very pervasive by distributing their "intelligence" into an amazing number of applications including many that had not existed before.

By choosing a microprocessor and supplier, an insoluble link between suppliers and manufacturers of PCs, smartphones, and all the products in which "embedded microprocessors" are the heart of, to determine their final functions is created.

In the nineties and even today, large companies for all practical purposes, connect their future to the success of their microprocessor suppliers.

Intel has been by far the greatest winner in this race to conquer the microprocessor market. Even Apple Computer, at a certain point, had to choose Intel to pursue its business objectives.

Marisa Bellisario visit Intel

Mrs. Marisa Bellisario, a Turin University graduated, was a highly recognized Italian manager. At Olivetti since the early sixties, she was regarded as the driving force, and at the time (1978), she was a key decision-maker as General Manager at Olivetti.

I had met Dr. Marisa Bellisario a couple of time and I remember how high her reputation inside that company was.

I knew that she was involved in all the technological and product choices and how expert she was even in the new technologies such as the use of semiconductor components.

Cover of the book on Dr. Bellisario

In June of that year, I received a call from Santa Clara informing me about a request from Enzo Torresi, head of the Olivetti's office in Cupertino, to organize a meeting between Intel and Marisa Bellisario to be held later that month at Intel during a tour that she was planning, to visit her suppliers.

All our current activities with that customer were really important and Jack Carsten asked for my participation at the meeting and to help him by informing Intel people about what was going on at Olivetti.

Ing. Enzo Torresi Olivetti Cupertino director

I confirmed my participation immediately and was eager for the opportunity to be part of the Intel staff in front of both Bellisario and Torresi. The simple fact was that on many previous occasions I had found myself in competition with the Olivetti office in Cupertino.

While I was 100% pushing Intel inside Olivetti the Cupertino Office had its objectives, often not in favor of what I was doing in Italy.

On top, I knew how important Mrs. Bellisario was and because she was a woman I had to make sure that no one at Intel would underestimate her. Then and even now, our technological world was and is male-dominated.

Bellisario was a top manager, practically an absolute rarity in a masculine market, and at the same time, she was responsible for a leading company whose key decisions about memories and microprocessors were on the table at that moment.

Jack Carsten, Intel World Sales Manager

The meeting was scheduled for June 29, 1978, at 9:00 AM and we had to be well prepared. It presented an excellent opportunity to reinforce our collaboration with Olivetti.

I arrived in California a couple of days before to spend some time with Intel executives and engineers to discuss Olivetti's business opportunities and then painted a picture of the issues and questions I thought Mrs. Bellisario would ask.

On the morning of the meeting, around 8 o'clock, we found ourselves in the meeting room, which was not very large and with a rectangular table at the center.

We discussed who should attend the meeting, in addition to Jack and myself, and it was decided that also the key product managers should be present.

We were all men but a very important woman was coming, how could we prove that we were not a male-dominated company?

So many years have passed now but I still remember how much I had been emphasizing the importance of that Lady, coming from Italy, that I knew in America was considered a leader in male-chauvinism.

I do believe that my effort induced my friend Jack Carsten to invent a solution that I could not even imagine.

At the very last minute, Jack called Miss Maria Ligeti, who was part of the memory group, a beautiful young woman of Hungarian origin, tall and with long black hair.

Jack thought that she seemed to be perfect as a participant to the meeting to show that Intel was far from being a sexist company and to be frank, I liked that movie too.

Close to the time of the appointment Jack, as a real team leader, had us sit around that table, positioning everyone strategically.

Jack sat at the head of the table on the opposite side of the door, Maria on his left, me on his right, ready to help him with the translation if necessary. The Intel product managers were split between the left and right sides of the table.

The seats at the other end of the table remained available to Mrs, Bellisario and her Olivetti staff.

Jack planned everything as a kind of battle to be won at any cost. I was a little worried because everything seemed to a bit too elaborate.

At 9 o'clock someone from the reception announced that Mrs. Bellisario and her staff had arrived and were heading towards our room. We all sat in silence waiting for the door to be opened.

Not more than 3 minutes passed, and Torresi, holding the door open, let in Mrs. Bellisario who elegantly dressed entered with firm step.

After a couple of steps and a quick look at the people present, not leaving us time to say hello and let her sit down, she pointed her finger at Maria and said: "Is she here because of me ?!" (That is, "Did you put on a female appearance because a woman was coming?").

The scene was really funny, and I bit my tongue to not laugh at seeing the faces of the bystanders, especially that of Jack, virtually frozen by a move that checkmated all of us.

That "wonderful" manager and Italian woman in a tenth of a second had understood everything and thrown a knock out punch.

I would have liked to get up and shake her hand, to congratulate her on the incredible effectiveness of those unexpected words that put her in a dominant position throughout the meeting.

Maria Ligeti in the center with her husband Gordie Campbell at their Ranch during a Thanksgiving day, a few years later

After a short pause and with a little embarrassment on our part, we welcomed everyone, and our guests sat with Mrs. Bellisario at the head of the table in front of Jack, and a list of topics to be discussed that morning were agreed.

I read on my agenda the name of all the participants to that meeting. Jack Carsten, Gordie Campbell, Tony Livingston, Jim Dodsen, and Dave House on the Intel side. Maria was a late addition. On the Olivetti side, there were, in addition to Enzo Torresi and Marisa Bellisario, Mazzola, Cafiero, John Alstrom, Bottino, and Jim Karas.

I took a lot of notes and I think it might be interesting to the reader that I'll highlight here some of what was asked by Olivetti. The questions were well thought out and were presented with great competence.

First of all, Intel was asked to disclose their plans for the next generation of microprocessors. Olivetti stated that the preparation and development of software required a long time and therefore they needed to know the plans of Intel.

Dave House offered to Olivetti Cupertino the collaboration of an engineer, Dave Gellatly, beginning in August.

Intel also confirmed their willingness to collaborate with Paul Rosenfield and Mazzola on a "memory manager control chip".

A further meeting was proposed with Mr. Casaglia to be held in July at Santa Clara.

A Non-Disclosure Agreement between Intel and Olivetti Cupertino was agreed on for any future collaboration between Santa Clara and Cupertino.

I should add that even at that meeting I was carrying my camera, but I did not ask to take a photo of the participants, as my habit, probably because I was afraid to receive a denial from Mrs. Bellisario. A great pity that I cannot show an image of that exceptional and historical meeting!

Intel and the Systems

We were now in the early seventies of the last century; Intel had abandoned the search for new markets like the quartz watches. For growth, they turned back to its well known industrial market, to build systems serving the same markets Intel had been serving with chips.

Having understood that out there existed ocean plenty of medium size companies willing to employ the new solid-state components but lacking needed design capabilities, Intel made a smart decision to provide them with ready to be used memory system solutions.

Those customers could greatly reduce their "time to market" by avoiding complicated and time-consuming design processes, thanks to fully assembled subsystems offered by Intel.

The idea for this project started in 1972: after all, it was a matter of connecting several chips on a single printed circuit board to create already tested and ready to use systems.

In this way, Intel's production of chips could be better exploited. By knowing the characteristics and therefore choosing them so that on the same board were mounted the chips with similar characteristics, Intel engineers were able to offer the best combination for any subsystem.

It was also possible to take advantage of those numerous chips that might have been discarded at the individual component level.

It became an extremely profitable market and added a competitive edge at Intel against those competitors that only were supplying chips.

This approach was extremely effective and would be used effectively at Intel for many years. Develop a new technology or product. Build the product into systems, to show the world how to do it and make the customer successful while at the same time teaching them how to do it themselves. In later years this grew into the Intel Field Applications Engineering organization, a resource non of Intel's competitors could match.

We will see in the chapter that will describe the Intel "Crush Program" how much this factor has been important.

The first assembled subsystems were memory boards, a natural development for Intel. The IN series was introduced to the market in the year 1972 and Italy we began to advertise and promote them, providing the needed after-sale assistance service.

These subsystems had a very positive welcome in Italy at companies much smaller than Olivetti or Honeywell. The Italian market was famous for the large number of medium size industries manufacturing operations in the automation field, telecommunication, and, in general, as suppliers to the main state-owned companies, supplying them specialized control systems.

MEMORY SYSTEMS

Type	Description	No. of Words (Per Card)	Word Length (Bits)	Access Time	Cycle Time	Supplies (V)	Page
in-10	RAM System	8K	8–18	275 ns	450 ns	+23.2 +19.7 +5	6-4
in-26	RAM System	4K	4–10	375 ns	375 ns	+5	6-6
in-40	RAM System	32K	8–18	330 ns	500 ns	+5 −5	6-8
in-50	RAM System	1K	2–10	100 ns	100 ns	+5	6-10
in-60	Serial Memory System	20K	8–10	500 ns	N/A	+5	6-12
in-64	Serial Memory System	88K	1–2	60 ns	N/A	+5	6-14
in-65	Serial Memory System	131K	8–9	550 ns	N/A	+17 +12 +5 −5	6-16
in-4711	PDP-11 Add-in	16K	16–18	150 ns	520 ns	From PDP-11	6-18
in-4716	Interdata 7/16 and 7/32 Add-in	16K	17	300 ns	1000 ns	+15 +5 −15	6-20
in-477	CRT Refresh Memory	16K	16	600 ns	850 ns	+12 +5 −5	6-22
in-481	8008, 8080 RAM Memory	16K	8	450 ns	600 ns	+12 +5 −9	6-24
	Custom Boards						6-26
	Cabinets						6-27
	Chassis						6-28
	Power Supplies						6-29
	Accessories						6-30

The IN10 series ranged from 1024 to 8192 words and from 8 to 18 bits per word

Intel and the Systems

An IN10 board with many Intel memory chips inserted

With the availability of microprocessors, the range of these subsystems expanded by including CPUs and peripheral boards.

The imm4 series and SBC (Single Board Computer) were born, real computers that a customer could insert into their machinery adding just their personalization via software.

Intel added an immense amount of support by supplying software, and training workshops.

MICROCOMPUTER MODULES

MCS-4/40™

Modules may be ordered individually. All modules are 8" wide, 6.18" high and use standard 100-pin connectors.

imm4-42 Central Processor Module
- This is a complete microcomputer system with the processor, program storage, data storage, and I/O in a single module.
- The heart of this module is Intel's 4004 single chip four-bit parallel processor — p-channel silicon gate MOS.
- Accumulator and sixteen working registers (4-bit).
- Subroutine nesting up to 3 levels.
- For development work, the CPU interfaces to standard

- 320 4-bit bytes of data storage (Intel 4002) expandable to 2560 x 4 using optional imm4-22 or imm4-24 modules.
- Four 4-line input ports and eight 4-line output ports expandable to 16 input and 48 output ports using optional imm4-60, imm4-22 or imm4-24 modules.
- Two phase crystal clock.

imm4-22 Instruction/Data Storage Module
- This microcomputer module has memory capacity iden-

MCS-80™

imm8-83 CPU Module

- Complete 8-bit parallel central processor module with system clocks, interface and control for memory, I/O ports, and real time interrupt.
- Utilizes Intel's high performance 8080 single chip n-channel microcomputer.
- 2.5 µsecond instruction execution time.
- 78 basic instructions including the entire 8008 instruction set.
- Direct addressing of up to 64K bytes of any speed ROM, PROM, or RAM memory.
- Unlimited subroutine nesting.
- Seven working registers — six 8-bit general purpose registers and an 8-bit accumulator.
- Separate 16-bit address bus, 8-bit output bus and 3 multiplexed 8-bit input busses for I/O input, memory input and interrupt data.
- Direct addressing of 256 input and 256 output ports.
- Multiple level real time interrupt capability.
- Direct memory access capability.
- All buses TTL compatible.

imm8-61 I/O Module

- Four 8-bit input and four 8-bit latching output ports.
- Directly compatible with imm8-83 central processor module.
- Integral asynchronous serial data communications capability and teletype interface.
- Jumper selectable transmission rates of 110, 1200 or 2400 baud.
- Crystal controlled clock.
- Capable of high speed serial communications to 9600 baud.
- TTL compatible.

imm8-63 Output Module

- Eight 8-bit latching output ports.
- Directly compatible with imm8-83 central processor module.
- Decoding provided for the selection of up to 256 individual output ports.
- TTL compatible.

MICROCOMPUTER MODULES

MCS-8™

imm8-82 Central Processor Module

- Intel's 8008 eight-bit parallel single chip CPU — p-channel silicon gate MOS.
- Accumulator and six 8-bit working registers.
- Subroutine nesting up to seven levels.
- Interface to 16K 8-bit bytes of PROM, ROM, or RAM via the PROM Memory Module and RAM Memory Module.
- Interface for expansion to eight 8-bit input ports and twenty-four 8-bit output ports, via the I/O and Output Modules.
- Interrupt capability.
- Two phase crystal clock.
- All module interfaces are TTL compatible.

imm8-60 Input/Output Module

- Four 8-bit input ports (32 lines).
- Four 8-bit data latching output ports (32 lines).
- One pair of ports for TTY communication.
- All input and output ports are TTL compatible.

imm8-62 Output Module

- Eight 8-bit data latching output ports (64 lines).
- All output ports are TTL compatible.

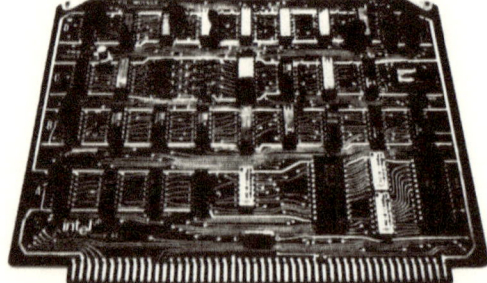

imm8-82 Central Processor Module

Intel and the Systems   125

MICROCOMPUTER MODULES

COMMON SYSTEM MODULES

imm6-26 PROM Memory Module
- Provides sockets for up to sixteen 1702A electrically programmable and erasable PROMs for a system's fixed program memory (maximum 4K bytes/module).
- For volume requirements, Intel 2048-bit mask programmed MOS ROMs (1302) may be substituted in the same module.

imm6-28 RAM Memory Module
- A 4K x 8 n-channel MOS memory system using Intel's 1024-bit Static RAM (2102).
- Address latching, data latching, and module select decoding are provided on the card.
- Provides program storage for up to 4K instructions.

imm6-70 Universal Prototype Module
- Accommodates 14, 16, 24, or 40 pin wire wrap sockets (maximum of 52 16-pin sockets).
- Provides breadboard capability for developing custom and specialized interface circuits.

imm6-72 Module Extender
- Extends Intellec modules out of card chassis for ease in test and system debugging.

imm6-76 PROM Programmer Module
- Provides all timing and level shifting circuitry for programming Intel's programmable and erasable 1702A PROMs.

OEM COMPUTER SYSTEMS

SBC 80/10 SINGLE BOARD COMPUTER

8080A Central Processing Unit

1 K bytes of read/write memory

Sockets for 4K bytes of programmable or masked read-only memory

48 Programmable I/O lines with sockets for interchangeable line drivers and terminators

Programmable Synchronous/Asynchronous communications interface with selectable teletype or RS232C compatibility.

Six interrupt request lines.

Bus drivers for memory and I/O expansion

Compatable with optional memory and I/O boards.

The SBC-80/10 is a member of Intel's complete line of OEM computer systems which take full advantage of Intel's LSI technology to provide economical, self-contained computer based solutions for OEM applications. The SBC-80/10 is a complete computer system on a single 6.75-by-12 inch printed circuit card. The CPU, system clock, read/write memory, non-volatile read-only-memory, I/O ports and drivers, serial communications interface, bus control logic and drivers all reside on the board.

Memory and I/O expansion may be achieved using standard Intel boards. Memory may be expanded to 65,536 bytes by adding user specified combinations of SBC-016 16K byte RAM boards, SBC-406 6K byte PROM boards, and SBC-416 16K PROM boards. Input/output capacity may be expanded to 63 8-bit input ports and 63 8-bit output ports using SBC-508 Input/Output boards. Each I/O board contains four 8-bit input ports and four 8-bit output ports. Memory and I/O may be expanded simultaneously (i.e. 4K bytes of RAM, 4K bytes of PROM, and 48 programmable I/O lines, and a USART) by using the SBC-104 Combination board. Expandable backplanes and card-cages are available to support multi-board systems.

OEM COMPUTER SYSTEMS

SBC-016 16K BYTE RAM MEMORY BOARD

SBC-80 RAM memory expansion through direct bus interface

16K byte read/write memory capacity

On-board hardware for refresh of all dynamic memory elements

Jumper selectable starting address for 16K contiguous addresses

Read/write data buffers

TTL compatible data, address, and command signal interface

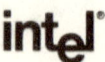

OEM COMPUTER SYSTEMS

SBC-104 COMBINATION MEMORY AND I/O EXPANSION BOARD

SBC 80 RAM and ROM/PROM memory expansion with parallel and serial I/O expansion through direct bus interface.

4K bytes of read/write memory.

Sockets for 4K bytes of programmable or masked read-only-memory.

48 programmable I/O lines with sockets for interchangeable line drivers and terminators.

Synchronous/Asynchronous communications interface with RS232C drivers and receivers.

Eight maskable interrupt request lines with a pending interrupt register.

1 ms interval timer.

OEM COMPUTER SYSTEMS

SBC-406 6K PROM EXPANSION BOARD

SBC 80 PROM/ROM expansion through direct bus interface

Sockets for up to 6K bytes of interchangeable Intel 1302 masked ROM or 8702A programmable and erasable PROM

Switches to enable or disable memory blocks

Switch selectable base addresses for a 2K and 4K memory block

Access time select switches to allow the selection of one of four versions of 8702A PROMs

Buffered address and data lines

MICROCOMPUTER SOFTWARE PRODUCTS

The following section contains information on Intel's Cross Software Products and User's Library. These cross products are all written in FORTRAN IV and are designed to run on a large computer system while generating code for or simulating one of Intel's microcomputers. All these products are also available on several computer timesharing services worldwide.

Included among these products are the PL/M$^{T.M.}$ compilers. The PL/M$^{T.M.}$ high level programming language was developed by Intel for the 8008 and 8080 microcomputers. Use of this language can significantly reduce programming time and costs.

A partial list of programs in the Intel microcomputer User's Library is also included. New programs are constantly being added to the library in a continuing effort to increase the size of the largest commercially available library of microcomputer programs in the world. You are encouraged to become a member to reap the benefits of the knowledge and experience of hundreds of users. Contributed programs are gratefully accepted.

Intel and the Systems

MICROCOMPUTER SOFTWARE PRODUCTS

The following section contains information on Intel's Cross Software Products and User's Library. These cross products are all written in FORTRAN IV and are designed to run on a large computer system while generating code for or simulating one of Intel's microcomputers. All these products are also available on several computer timesharing services worldwide.

Included among these products are the PL/M$^{T.M.}$ compilers. The PL/M$^{T.M.}$ high level programming language was developed by Intel for the 8008 and 8080 microcomputers. Use of this language can significantly reduce programming time and costs.

A partial list of programs in the Intel microcomputer User's Library is also included. New programs are constantly being added to the library in a continuing effort to increase the size of the largest commercially available library of microcomputer programs in the world. You are encouraged to become a member to reap the benefits of the knowledge and experience of hundreds of users. Contributed programs are gratefully accepted.

MCS-40 CROSS ASSEMBLER

Accepts all 4004 and 4040 instructions
Conditional assembly capability
Full macro facility
Hexadecimal or BNPF object code formats

Written in ANSI standard FORTRAN IV
Comprehensive user documentation
Instantly available on worldwide timesharing services

MCS-8™ CROSS ASSEMBLER

Accepts all 8008 instructions
Conditional assembly capability
Full macro facility
Hexadecimal or BNPF object code formats

Written in ANSI standard FORTRAN IV
Comprehensive user documentation
Instantly available on worldwide timesharing services

4004/4040 SIMULATOR

Simulates all 4004/4040 machine instructions
Accepts output from MAC40, the Intel® 4004/4040 Cross Assembler
Contains extensive symbolic debugging capabilities
Written in ANSI standard FORTRAN IV
Instantly available on worldwide timesharing services

COMMAND CAPABILITIES:
Set breakpoints
Trace program execution
Dump and modify memory
Examine and modify registers
Examine and set I/O ports

8008 SIMULATOR

Simulates all 8008 machine instructions
Accepts output from PL/M™ compiler or MAC8 cross assembler
Comprehensive debug features

Written in FORTRAN IV
Instantly available on worldwide timesharing services
Comprehensive user documentation

8080 SIMULATOR

Simulates all 8080 machine instructions
Accepts output from PL/M™ compiler or MAC80 Cross Assembler

Written in FORTRAN IV
Instantly available on worldwide timesharing services
Comprehensive user documentation

Intel and the Systems

PL/M™ HIGH LEVEL PROGRAMMING LANGUAGE
MCS-8™ AND MCS-80™ CROSS COMPILERS

Reduces program development time and cost
Improves product reliability and eases maintenance
Available for 8008 and 8080
Comprehensive user documentation

Hexadecimal or BNPF object code formats
Written in ANSI standard FORTRAN IV
Instantly available on worldwise timesharing services

MICROCOMPUTER SOFTWARE LIBRARY
USER'S PROGRAM LIBRARY

The Intel Microcomputer User's Library is a collection of programs, subroutines, procedures and macros written by users of Intel's 4004, 4040, 8008 or 8080 microcomputers. Thanks to customer contributions to the User's Library, Intel is now able to make these programs available to all users of Intel microcomputers. By taking advantage of the availability of these general purpose routines, the microcomputer design engineer and programmer can save many hours of programming and debugging.

A complete, documented listing of each program, procedure or macro in the user's library is sent to each member. This includes information on the program environment, required hardware and software, subroutine calling sequences and memory requirements. As new programs are submitted to the User's Library, they will be sent to all members. Strict documentation standards will be maintained to assure the usability of each library program by every interested member. Several of the available programs are listed in this brochure.

MICROCOMPUTER SOFTWARE LIBRARY
PARTIAL PROGRAM INDEX-4-BIT USERS LIBRARY

TITLE	FUNCTION
Cross Assembler on PDP-8	Performs symbolic assembly for 4004 assembly language programs. The assembler runs on a DEC PDP-8 minicomputer.

PARTIAL PROGRAM INDEX-8-BIT USERS LIBRARY
8-BIT MICROCOMPUTER SOFTWARE LIBRARY

TITLE	FUNCTION
Save/Restore CPU State on an Interrupt	Saves the CPU registers and flags to memory at the start of interrupt processing and restores the CPU registers and flags after the interrupt has been processed.

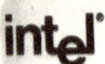

MICROCOMPUTER TRAINING
MICROCOMPUTER WORKSHOPS

Microcomputers are being used in hundreds of applications from simple controllers to complex data processing systems. To enable users to bring microcomputers into their applications, Intel is offering a selection of 3 and 4 day workshops that are designed to provide you with the "tools" for making optimum use of Intel microcomputers in system development.

PL/M LANGUAGE WORKSHOP — TRAINING

COURSE OBJECTIVE: This workshop will prepare the student for writing and debugging PL/M programs using lecture, demonstration, and laboratory "hands-on" experience in operating PL/M interactively from a high-speed, time-shared computer terminal.

Intel and the Systems

TIMEKEEPING CIRCUITS

 **5810A**

SINGLE CHIP LCD TIME/SECONDS/DATE WATCH CIRCUIT

- On Chip Voltage Multiplier Provides 4.5V For Driving 3½ Digit Field Effect Display
- Only Two Switches Required For Complete Operation Of The Watch
- Operates With 32.768 kHz Quartz Crystal
- Anti-Bounce Protection On Switch Inputs
- AM/PM Indication When Setting Time

Thank these SBCs in 1976 we managed to close a large order at Urmet Spa, a small company in Rome supplying subsystems to state-owned SIP, the national telephone company, a kind of Italian ATT.

In a public tender, Urmet won a contract to supply about one thousand control units to be built and delivered to the large client in a few months.

There was no way for that small company to design and to produce what intel and SBCs offered. We saved them.

I had begun talking to Mr. D'Attoma and Mr. Rimini, the owners, about the supply of various Intel chips, but as soon as I out their schedule requirements, an impossibility, I suggested they should forget our components and to have a look our SBC.

Needless to say that they wanted a few samples overnight and tested them just as quickly they could see a solution to a problem immediately. Afterword, they confirmed that their schedule requirements were keeping them awake at night.

The price negotiation was quite difficult and I was back and forward with Jim Lally and Hal Feeney to adjust our offer and to close that huge order.

When pricing and technical specs were agreed upon, Urmet produced a few prototypes for SIP approval, and following the positive acceptance the big order was signed.

I should say that despite the complexity of the SBC boards compared to a memory chip I found less technical troubles with that delivery than with chips to my large customers.

During a visit to the US, Jim Lally confessed to me that order was the largest single order received by his department from Europe and that he was extremely grateful to me for that.

In the seventies, Intel produced other systems like the SDK cards, which could be considered a kind of personal computer on board but at that time Intel did not spend time thinking about that market.

Intel and the Systems 133

The first of the series was the SDK80 practically a partially assembled 8-bit PC with an 8080 CPU, but no software. This Kit became available in mid-1974.

8080 SYSTEM DESIGN KIT SDK-80

Complete single board microcomputer system including CPU, memory and I/O
Easy to assemble kit-form
High-performance (2 μs instruction cycle)

Interfaces directly with most terminals (75-4800 baud)
Large wire-wrap area for custom interfaces
Extensive system monitor software in ROM
PC board format and power, compatible with Intellec®MDS

The 8080 System Design Kit (SDK-80) is a complete, single board, microcomputer system in kit form. It contains all necessary components, including resistors, caps, crystal and miscellaneous hardware to complete construction. Included is a pre-programmed ROM that contains the system monitor for general software utilities and system diagnostics.

All that is required for operation are power supplies and a suitable terminal; TTY, CRT, etc., (level conversions and baud rate generation included on board).

The SDK-80 is an inexpensive, high-performance prototype system that has designed-in flexibility for simple interface to the users application.

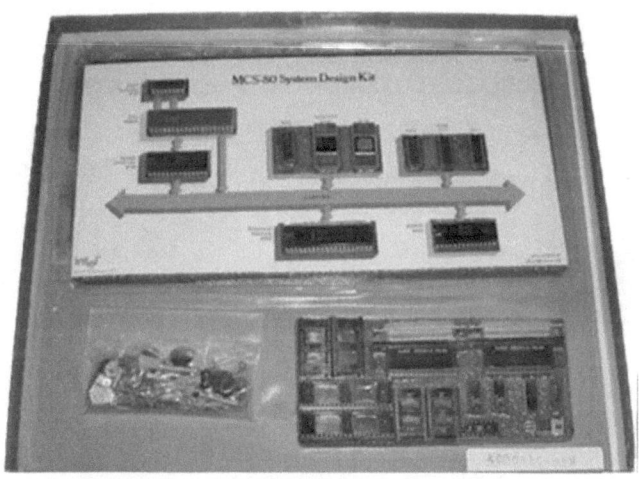

SDK80 System Design Kit introduced the 1984

Important has been the "Development Systems" which were real computers dedicated to the environment of system designers.

Based on the recent microprocessors, they had a great part to help our clients to reach their market quickly and to help designers to implement their products with Intel CPU.

The Intellec line could emulate a microprocessor and allow engineers to develop their software.

In Italy, we sold many such "Intellec Systems" to small and medium-sized companies so they were able to complete their projects quickly and easily.

The need to serve a market that required new tools, services, and education led Eledra to create two new dedicated structures.

A new logistics, to take care of the increased number of new products, new after-sales services, to take care of maintenance and warranty and new specialized personnel.

Eledra Systems and Edelektron were founded in Milan to take the burden of supporting the sales force selling Intel products.

Intellec, development systems for computer designers

We sold many Intellec systems to small and medium-sized companies and soon after we could profit from chips volume sales.

We could book these orders because we had the right skills. Moreover, some large companies in the refinery, transport and other sectors entrusted our Eledra Systems Spa, founded in 1974, with the complete design of their control systems.

UNA REALIZZAZIONE ELEDRA SYSTEMS

Vista generale delle raffinerie dall'alto di un serbatoio della stazione di caricamento

SERBATOI PRODOTTI PETROLIFERI
• cinque serbatoi da 1000 m³ per benzina normale, super e gasolio
• gruppo pompe composto da 12 pompe da 120 m³/h

CORSIA DI CARICAMENTO DI AUTOBOTTI E AUTOCHILOLITRICHE

TUTTO IL SETTORE TRASPORTI PUO' USUFRUIRE DI SOLUZIONI L'INDUSTRIA PETROLIFERA ITALIANA CONTIENE I COSTI

Some projects we have made for important Italian industries

Training customers about the use of such new semiconductor components required the development of a vast amount of technical documentation and the organization of specialized courses and seminars. To manage all these specific activities we founded Edelektron Srl, a publishing company.

Milan: Edelektron Srl, first Headquarters

Edelektron office and conference room

Milan: Eledra Systems Spa first Headquarters

Eledra Systems laboratories

Intel and the Systems

I would like to conclude this chapter by reporting the programs of three workshops that Intel implemented as regular products that, we distributors, were asked to supply to our clients as they were standard products.

TRAINING

SERIES 3000 WORKSHOP

COURSE OBJECTIVE: This workshop will provide the student with an in-depth understanding of the Series 3000 family through the use of lecture and demonstration. Microprogramming and design examples are presented.

COURSE OUTLINE:

DAY 1

Introduction
a. Introduction to Microprogramming
b. The Series 3000 Component Family
c. Series 3000 System Overview

CPU Design Example
a. CPU System Requirements
b. Architecture of a CPU
c. Developing a Macro-instruction Set
d. Interrupt Handling
e. Microprogram Mapping

DAY 2

Design Techniques
a. Conditional Clocking
b. K-Bus
c. Micro-instruction Field Extension
d. Micro-subroutines
e. Pipelining
f. Timing Analysis

Controller Design Example
a. Disc Controller System Requirements
b. Architecture of a Disc Controller
c. Microprogram Implementation

DAY 3

Development Support
a. Introduction to CROMIS, the Series 3000 Cross Micro-Assembler
b. MDS-800 Microcomputer Development System
c. ICE-30 In-Circuit Emulator
d. ROM Simulator
e. Demonstration

PL/M LANGUAGE WORKSHOP

TRAINING

COURSE OBJECTIVE: This workshop will prepare the student for writing and debugging PL/M programs using lecture, demonstration, and laboratory "hands-on" experience in operating PL/M interactively from a high-speed, time-shared computer terminal.

COURSE OUTLINE:

DAY 1

Introduction
a. Overview of PL/M
b. Preview of Course

Definitions
a. Symbols
b. Identifiers
c. Reserved Words
d. Comments
e. Data Elements
f. Expressions
g. Statements
h. Declarations

Data Elements
a. Variables
b. Subscripted Variables
c. Data Type
d. Constants

DAY 2

Review

Procedures
a. Declaration
b. Invocation
c. Program Construction

Data References
Statement Labels
Unconditional Transfers
Compile-Time Macro Processing
Input/Output Processing
Simulating an 8080 System
Laboratory
a. Compile Programs

DAY 3

Review
Memory Mapping
Assembly Language Interface
Interrupt Processing
Predeclared Variables and Procedures
a. LENGTH and LAST
b. Condition Code
c. Memory Vector
d. TIME Procedure
e. Type Transfer
f. Decimal Arithmetic
g. Shifts and Rotates
Laboratory

My Intel Story

TRAINING

MCS-80/ICE-80 WORKSHOP

COURSE OBJECTIVE: This workshop will prepare the student to design and develop a system using the Intel® 8080 microprocessor through the use of lecture, demonstration, and laboratory "hands-on" experience with the Intellec MDS development system and ICE-80.

COURSE OUTLINE:

DAY 1
Introduction
a. Microprocessor System Fundamentals
   Function/Organization/Programming
b. Introduction to the 8080
   1. Basic System
      a) CPU
      b) Memory
      c) Input/Output: (Programmed/Interrupt/DMA)
   2. Programming Model
c. Languages
   1. Machine Code
   2. Assembly Language
   3. PL/M

Instructions
a. Input/Output
b. Register/Memory Reference
c. Control/Arithmetic

The Intellec MDS
a. Function/Operation
b. System Monitor

The Text Editor

DAY 2
The Macro Assembler
a. Syntax/Pseudo-Instructions
b. Operation

System Timing
a. Instruction
b. Clock
c. Address/Data

Input/Output Programming
Subroutines
a. Invocation
b. Stack Memory
c. Parameter Passing

Teletype Programming Requirements
The Interrupt System
a. Definition
b. RST Instruction
c. Service Subroutines

Laboratory
a. Using the Assembler
b. Program Assembly and Execution

DAY 3
Branch Table
a. Application
b. Construction

Direct Load/Store Instructions
System Monitor Debugging Function
System Design Process
a. Memory and I/O Requirements
b. Bus Control
c. Clocks
d. Hardware/Software Trade-offs

Additional Development Aids
Laboratory
a. Program Assembly and Execution
b. PROM Programming

DAY 4
What is "In Circuit Emulation"
ICE-80 Description
a. Functional Block Diagram
b. Theory of Operation

ICE-80 Laboratory
a. Operating the ICE-80
b. Emulating an 8080 Based System

32-bit CPU: the disastrous iAPX432

In the second half of the seventies, I found myself in a kind of a mysterious operation of the kind of the "007 secret agents" of the movie.

In the field, the war among the CPU contenders was red like hot iron, and any kind of news, true or false, was creating anxieties about who would win that race.

Zilog, Motorola, Mostek, and other newcomers were talking about their future products even if they were still just on paper.

As an Intel partner and, more, a great Intel believer I was concerned whether the Intel scientists could keep up with the avalanche of announces

I could not believe that Intel wasn't doing something big to react and win that important race and help us on the front line, to fight all those competitors claiming to be ahead of us.

I don't remember exactly when, but the fact is that during one of my visits to Santa Clara I heard something about a big and top-secret Intel operation going on in Oregon.

I wasn't aware of any Intel factory there and so I started to investigate what seemed to be a strictly confidential development that only top Intel managers were allowed to know.

After so many years all of us involved in the Intel business know all the details of the Intel engineer's desire to jump ahead of the CPU race by designing a new 32-bit microprocessor named "Intel Advanced Performance Architecture" programmable in high-level languages like ADA compiler.

The design was a complete departure from the 8080 structure and not compatible with what later on would become the x86 path.

Now we know that the Oregon project somehow failed for the simple reason that they were trying to implement in silicon an

Object-Oriented mainframe architecture far too advanced to be constrained in one silicon chip.

I didn't get any detail about the coming specs of the iAPX32 (later 432) but I was sure it would be successful. Being the iAPX32 an Intel Idea. I pushed our Eledra Systems division to start working with an Ada compiler which would be the focus compiler to write code in for the iAPX32 and to investigate what was published by the United States Department of Defense on that subject.

As before, we wanted to be ready in advance of our market opportunities by publishing Italian documentation and books, even before our American friends.

At the moment the only information I could get on the project was regarding the ADA language and we hurried to publish a book on the ADA compiler in Italy on behalf of the coming iAPX432.

1977. First ADA compiler manual published in Italy

While I was dreaming about the coming new chip to fight back Intel CPU competitors, I was thinking about the change of mind of

32-bit CPU: the disastrous iAPX432

Intel managers that were now convinced that the CPU game was an important battle to win.

Intel started the CPU market in 1971 with the first 4-bit microprocessor created by Ted Hoff, Stan Mazor, and Federico Faggin. In the beginning, all the efforts of the Intel management were focussed on the memory market, their workhorse.

I clearly remember the disappointment of Federico Faggin and his discussions with Les Vadasz and Andy Grove to find the resources he needed to design a new microprocessor, his resignation, and the creation of Zilog when his requests for funds were turned down.

Zilog, founded by Ralph Ungermann and Federico Faggin, was financed by Exxon, which held majority shareholding and by the Japanese designer Matsushita Shima that came to Intel from the Japanese company Busicam to help the design of the first 4-bit microcomputer kit.

In just 8 months Zilog succeeded in bringing the Z80, a microprocessor superior to the Intel 8080 to the market which became the market leader in the 8-bit market for its exceptional performance.

It was then that Intel managers began to realize that they could not lose focus on a market that they had started.

The nascent Personal Computer market was beginning, even if in the early phase where hobbyists were designing and building their computers. Hobbyist, did not, however, use either the Intel or Zilog CPUs, but the cheaper 6502 produced by MOS Technology and its different versions.

Even the giants of the sector like Motorola and Texas Instruments competed with Intel making the "Design In" important above everything else in the industrial market.

The competition among all these manufacturers was developing towards the new generations of CPU, first the 16-bit and then the 32-bit processor generations that were still secret, in their development phase.

One of the biggest nightmares in Silicon Valley companies' directions was keeping key technical personnel who were developing these new products.

Many of those technologists and engineers were starting their own companies or leaving their well-paid jobs to join companies where they were better paid and had technical challenges they found their companies were not giving them. The results were difficult for the company they were leaving because of their departure and also created new competitors such as Zilog.

While we waiting for new announcements from Intel, our major competitors, Motorola and Zilog, were bringing new products to market such as the 6800, 68000, Z80, and Z8000. Customers were struggling with this around the world.

Motorola, with its large production capacity and microprocessors with a better graphics interface, were perceived to offer better solutions than Intel.

Of course, even in Italy, that competition was present. Olivetti at the end of the seventies did their evaluation for its future uses, the three 16-bit microprocessors from Motorola and Zilog, in addition to Intel.

I was continually following the analyzes that my client was carrying out, both from a technical point of view and from cost forecasts.

This strong interest continued for at least a year, partly because I had understood that Olivetti, with its evaluations, planned to enter the Personal Computer market that had been neglected until then.

The great success of the Apple II in America with millions of pieces sold and the presence of those computers also in Italy had pushed Olivetti to review their position towards what they considered a hobby market.

IBM still had no interest in developing this market, but surely would have been the right choice for a great manufacturer and a big international like Olivetti to partner with. It was also clear to me that from a performance standpoint, Motorola was a winner and I still believe that today.

Needless to say, I waited with some anxiety news from Oregon and did not understand the silence.

To win an order with the Intel 8086 against the best 68000 Motorola, I needed something more than what we had at hand.

I wondered why with all those resources lavished on that project why was Intel waiting to communicate something to the market.

If we had waited too long, the competition would have won the few available market opportunities and made the situation irreversible for Intel.

I would have discovered a long time later, that my considerations were also discussed within Intel, as the marketing manager and my dear friend Bill Davidow later revealed to me.

I do not know who conceived the development of the new CPU in Oregon, but I am convinced that the project was conceived by Andy Grove and Les Vadasz: worried by the resignation of Faggin and consequent from the foundation of the competitor Zilog, they also convinced Bob Noyce and Gordon Moore but Intel historians seldom say anything about it.

It seems credible to me that Andy Grove had deemed it necessary to make an ambitious technological leap forward to make the pursuit of competition difficult or impossible.

The difficulties and delays associated with this ultimately unsuccessful project frustrated the Intel sales operations and, indeed, had the same effect on me.

While the microprocessor marketing organization had a clear focus that "standardization" over the various generations of microprocessors should deliver upwards compatibility to help industrial customers, Intel engineers dreamed of the creation of products with "star" specifications.

At the end the expensive program in Oregon was unsuccessful. While a product was ultimately delivered, it was too late and missed being an overwhelming performance success. Worse, it put Intel at great risk, and me too.

Despite all this, during the year 1979 Intel managed to overturn many of the difficulties the products faced. This situation was not because of a technology leap, but through a brilliant marketing operation internally called "Operation Crush". It was conceived by Bill Davidow and involved the whole company. Any necessary resource was made available. In the field, that involved me and my company for all efforts concerning customers in Italy. We will focus on Operation Crush in the next chapter.

"Crush Program": a masterpiece of marketing

To understand what happened at Intel during the year 1980 and how the company has been saved from a looming disaster, we need to evaluate how Intel was positioned at that time on the microprocessor market.

Today not many people could imagine that Intel, now a world leader in the microchip business, at that time lost the technological leadership and was near to a market disaster.

For all that I have written to this point, Intel was a factory designing and manufacturing semiconductor components and in a decade has been able to exploit the best technologies available to produce memory chips of various sizes.

All of its commercial force and even my Eledra directed their efforts to win designs, "design-ins", in major industries, and to have its memory chips on their printed circuits boards.

Once in production, these industries repaid the hard work of "design-in" with their large production orders.

The Personal Computer market had just been born and had not been touched by Intel. Apple Computer used components produced by other suppliers.

I cannot forget the visit report of the Intel salesman in charge at Apple Computer in Cupertino. In his report, he wrote: "A company not worth spending time about".

And even the top managers, like Moore and Noyce, didn't care about the hobbyist market. They were of scientific origin and essentially leaders in the semiconductor technology and were not marketing oriented, in my opinion.

Andy Grove also belonged to the same technological world and his excellent books on semiconductor technology illustrated his scientific mentality.

While this may have been a winning approach in the beginning, but 20 years later, the market and the competition were dictating the rules, jeopardizing the existence of the whole company.

Intel technologies had become widespread but it was marketing and Bill Davidow who saved it and not the ambitions of an advanced IAPX 432 described in the previous chapter.

In retrospect, I can say with absolute certainty that the year 1979 had been a most difficult for Intel and was the foundation for what happened later, when in the 1986 Andy Grove, the just named president, made the incredible decision to abandon the memory market and to focus the company entirely on microprocessors.

At the end of the seventies, Intel revenues were based on the supplying large volumes of various memory chips, mainly to industries producing large computers, telecommunication equipment, and automation industries, markets that would soon become the prey of Japanese producers like NEC, Hitachi, and Toshiba that were capable of selling those memories at very low prices.

While the sale of microprocessors was growing rapidly, profitability and volumes did not compensate for the decrease in memory chips revenues and the pressure on the sales force was to limit the loss of memory orders huge. Intel offered the microprocessor as a bonus if the kit of components under discussion with a client was "fat", i.e. with many memory chips.

The microprocessor was used as an incentive to compete with memory makers!

I was personally involved in implementing this, almost desperate, battle in that market environment.

Moreover, even the microprocessor market invented by Intel was under heavy fire by two fearful competitors, Motorola and Zilog.

Virtually Intel looked like a lion on an island in the middle of a lake, while on all sides, various crocodiles were trying to bite it.

"Crush Program": a masterpiece of marketing

As always, when our life seems jeopardized is the moment when the best solutions are found to save ourselves.

In this case, Intel turned to its marketing battalion, the organization that was in the front row on what was now a real battle of which I was part, a battle almost lost before it began.

There was no time to think about new technologies, projects in Oregon, to study some new product like the memories of 1970. Intel was already at war and had to fight back now and with the weapons, it had at hand.

The most important weapon that differentiated Intel from its competitors was marketing. Marketing, the same marketing that in the beginning, top Intel executives considered an ancillary entity.

And my Eledra and I were at that time a small contributor to the Intel marketing but now I can talk about what happened that year as a real witness.

I strongly believe that understanding what happened that year is one of the best marketing lessons for any company, even the most modern.

I will do my best to be precise in my descriptions by reading the many notes I have collected from my calendars and remembering the many meetings with the various Intel managers who were involved in this aggressive project.

It all started with an analysis of the long list of "Design-in" lost around the world against competitors who were producing next-generation 16-bit microprocessors.

The cruel reality showed that even the 8-bit CPU market started by Intel a few years before with its 8008, 8080, and 8085, had been overtaken by the excellent Motorola 6800 and Zilog Z80.

Even so, the 8-bit market sales-wise was still managing quite well for Intel and in Italy too we were able to maintain a dominant position.

Things were rapidly deteriorating; the microprocessor market was mature and become aware of the better performance of our competitors.

Field sales reports were reporting how many customers, nine out of ten, were also moving from 8 bits CPU to 16 bits CPU and were also choosing the Motorola 68000 or the Zilog Z8000.

Even though those choices did not mean an immediate loss of revenue, what was going on had to be considered the premise for the loss of future volume orders, a short-term risk.

In Italy, in mid-1979 Olivetti, in Luigi Mercurio's design group, with whom I was in daily contact, was evaluating the top line of Intel processor and also the Motorola 68000 and the Zilog Z8000.

My doubt was whether they were willing to deal with the obscure Oregon project or look to something else.

Any suspicion was thwarted when I was told that the entire Intel sales organization, the most qualified distributors including Eledra with its salesmen and FAE (Field Application Engineers), were invited to be part of a very secret and revolutionary marketing effort, internally called "Operation Crush".

The aim of that project, with the mysterious name that seemed to fit better with the Allied landings in Normandy, had to be to destroy the competition.

It turned out that the "Crush" designation, used internally, came from a football (American Football) team, the Denver Broncos. Their extremely successful defensive unit was called "Orange Crush", orange because of the color of their uniforms and "Crush" because of their success in crushing their competitor's offense.

I received a bundle of documents illustrating the plan of attack and with which weapons we had to present ourselves to customers.

"Crush Program": a masterpiece of marketing

For the most important customers in the world, including Olivetti, a special force of "green berets" was ready to take off from Santa Clara to any destination.

Even the Intel senior executives were available wherever it seemed useful to be present with their prestige.

It looked like a declaration of war on competition and a call to arms from all the organizations, those inside Intel and the external ones like us.

The plan established a series of focus clients in Italy the Olivetti was listed with actions planned for autumn 1980. The moment coincided with the decisions that Olivetti had to make for their new projects.

Project Crush was initiated in November of 1979 by the executive staff based on a telex received from Don Buckhout one of our east coast sales managers. He identified that we were losing design wins to Motorola and Zilog. By the new year, there was an approved, by Intel executives, Intel Field sales, and budgeted plan. The program kicked off worldwide in January of 1980 with concurrent sales training in the US, Europe, and Japan.

I discussed the issue personally in Milan with Tom Lawrence, then president of Intel Europe, and we prepared specific actions for other Italian industries, involving Eledra Systems and Edelektron.

My concern with Olivetti I will deal in detail in the next chapter. Our magazine ETN published an insert translating into Italian a document that Intel produced in support field sales and this program.

An incredible fact is that in my recent conversation with Dane Elliot, former Intel, who now cares for the company's history, as Intel Alumni Network (IAN) Historian, asked me for a copy for the Computer History Museum and IAN historical publications. I'm the only one in the world to have some of the historical Intel documents. Sixteen pages of these documents, translated into Italian, are included below.

My Intel Story

Extract of the 16 pages of the public document on the "Crash Program

These documents were only the public part of the Crush Campaign. The aim was to represent Intel no longer as a manufacturer of components but as a well-rounded manufacturer,

"Crush Program": a masterpiece of marketing   151

with computers for designing (development systems), prototype boards, software, and support staff.

We wanted to underline the "power" of the company delivering what a customer needed, a real partner for their future development, and not just a component supplier.

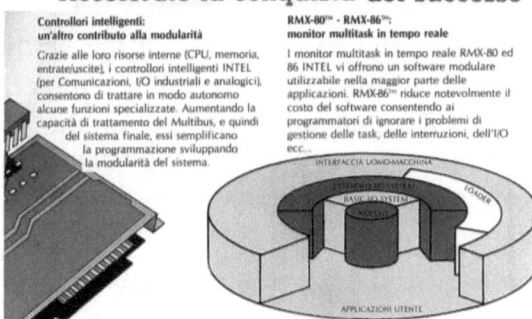

It is emphasized that Intel is providing a complete range of services

Special care was reserved for the largest clients. For these important prospects and under a Non-Disclosure Agreement, Intel revealed a preview for its plan to produce future generations of microprocessors, all software, upwards compatible between generations that would reduce time to market and investments for all Intel partners.

This presentation was the prelude to what is still today the success of Intel in the world and that is the X86 technology, the heart of its microprocessors.

In practice it was anticipation, of what the Intel technology would deliver after the 8086, making believers of our customers. Intel was revealing internal plans for the next generation 186, 286 processors. This would then lead to the 386, 486, Pentium, all backward software compatible, microprocessors which still had to be designed.

ALL WAS A MARKETING PROPOSAL SPREAD EVERYWHERE, EVEN BEFORE THE ENGINEERS HAD PROVEN THEIR FEASIBILITY! IT COMMITTED INTEL TO CONTINUE TO INNOVATE AS WE HAVE SEEN THEY DID AND CONTINUE TO DO!

The marketing group had identified their trump card to overturn the disastrous situation that was not about technology but had to deal with what the market was looking for. The engineers then were forced to produce what they promised and they succeed in doing so.

I consider this the best example in the world that many companies, even Italian ones, should study and understand.

The internal documentation ended with this message: "WE HAVE TO STOP PROPOSING COMPONENTS AND TO PRESENT INTEL AS THE DEPENDABLE COMPANY THAT OFFERS LONG-TERM SOLUTIONS".

The battle was shifted from component-level to a much higher level of a global business partnership looking into the distant future.

It was a desperate but well-conceived and executed operation for survival by trusting that the Intel engineers would then be able to implement what they promised.

"Crush Program": a masterpiece of marketing

At Intel sales and marketing people had made very clear what the market wanted: to save on the costly development of proprietary software and to reduce their time to market. This new Intel approach fulfilled that need.

Another winning aspect focusing on rising the decision-making level at the client-side. It was shifted from the laboratory and designing people to the general management, where competitors had many more problems getting access to.

Intel forced companies to make political decisions and not technical just ones. Intel was no longer fighting against some modest technical parameter but forcing our clients to make decisions that would affect their success for years to come.

Everything worked well, indeed very well. I was informed by Bill Davidow that the Crush Program expected to win at least 1,000 design wins with our customers within twelve months. At the end of the year, Intel won many more designs than originally forecasted, in fact, more than 2000.

The future of Intel was thus saved not by-products that did not exist but by a simple idea and commitment written on paper!

Motorola and Zilog, the direct competitors, could not attempt to counter this disruptive action in time. Intel had long been regarded as a "system company" by its sales force and the people in the field, like the Eledra salesmen and me, were ready for that battle.

Motorola was a much bigger as a company, but its components division was only a small part of the company lacking this kind of know-how and was unable to deliver to their field sales force in time.

In conclusion, "Operation Crush" was a marketing masterpiece, on the cutting edge of daring and, as the maxim says: "risk sometimes pays" and here it paid off extremely well!

I should mention now that Motorola in the year 1980 tried hard to get Eledra and me on their side. I received an invitation to visit their factory at 5005 East Mc Dowell Rd, Austin, Texas to meet Gary Tooker, Vice President of the semiconductor division. I accepted their offer to meet at their Austin Texas facility and in addition to Gary Tooker, I also met Joe Jordan, head of distribution and Chuck Kelly, responsible for Europe.

The visit was very interesting, and the size of the factory impressed me quite a bit. I also spoke with various product managers like Ian Le Maire for microprocessors and I must say that they did everything to show me how successful they were against Intel which they knew was part of my portfolio in Italy.

1980, Austin, Texas. Visiting Motorola Semiconductors

Surely it would have been an excellent line for Eledra and not so much for microprocessors or memories, but their vast components catalog. I did not sign the agreement because Intel vetoed adding Motorola to my product mix. I would never, even remotely have thought about giving up the Intel line and replacing it with Motorola even if they offered me gold mines.

In conclusion and returning to the "Crush Program", all of Intel and myself managed a masterpiece of marketing at the limit of reckless and, as the maxim says: "risk sometimes pays" and here has been repaid and far more than we could think!

In the next chapter, I will report what happened in Italy and at Olivetti.

The success of the Crush Program at Olivetti ... but!

I will describe for the first time how the crush program succeeded in Italy and how Olivetti, the largest client in the country, behaved and ultimately lost a great opportunity.

The Intel Crush Program, as illustrated in the previous chapter, strongly involved me as personally responsible of the main Italian targets of the program. During the year 1980 Olivetti designers were involved heavily in creating systems based on a 16-bit third-generation microprocessor.

I had no idea that their projects also included the design of a Personal Computer but from the many technical requests for information about Intel components at a certain point, I started to suspect that a PC was on the process of being prototyped.

Also, Olivetti Cupertino Center was very proactive toward Intel Santa Clara and very demanding for samples and information. My main Olivetti contacts in Ivrea were Ing. Luigi Mercurio, chief designer, Ing. Corrado Santerini, research center buyer, and Ing. Eugenio Sacerdote, production purchasing manager.

At midyear, I learned quite clearly that the Motorola 68000 was considered to be favored from the technical performance point of view.

This fact did not surprise me; even in the meetings at Intel and talking to other Intel distributors this superiority of the Motorola chip was a proven fact. To counter-attack from Motorola we began to take advantage of the Intel "Crush Initiative". Specifically with a series of actions, carried out with Tom

Lawrence, president of Intel Europe, Lou Calcagno, at that time in charge of Intel Italy and me.

We could access all Intel human resources like Ed Gelbach, Stan Mazor, Jack Carsten, Dave House, and their internal staff to achieve our goal of eliminating Motorola from contention.

In Europe, another problem did arise for large users, which is the "second source" and not only for the CPUs but for all the sensitive components, without which it would be difficult for these large users to go into production.

In the US the second source was at that time AMD and in Europe Siemens, but with the latter the relationship with Intel was quite difficult. To eliminate this obstacle that could jeopardize our project with Olivetti, I suggested the Italian SGS (Società Generale Semiconduttori) as a potential second source for the Intel components.

SGS was well known by Noyce and Moore with whom the company had a partnership during the time of Fairchild. I Checked with Ed Gelbach to see if Intel would be willing to negotiate this partnership and having received a "go ahead", I met the SGS management at Agrate (Italy) to probe their interest in the opportunity. I received a more than a favorable level of interest.

The SGS managers went to Santa Clara where they met Ed Gelbach and, I believe, also Bill Davidow and Jack Carsten. I thought that the agreement could be reached, but sometime later I received a call from Ed Gelbach that informed me that SGS had not proposed anything back and the agreement faded.

In the same period, exactly the beginning of September 1979, Enzo Torresi from Olivetti in Cupertino, confirmed to Intel my regular reports that Olivetti was close to a final decision about what 32 bit CPU to be used for future projects.

Through my daily contacts I was aware that the group headed by Luigi Mercurio was 100% in favor of Intel and that no further actions were required at that point, more, I knew, however, of all the personal fights at Olivetti so I suggested that the team should be extremely careful of the local Italian politics.

Intel Santa Clara, clearly anxious not to lose the customer, decided to send a well equipped technical mission to Ivrea, headed by Dr. Lucio Lanza, at the time employed at Intel as expert systems design engineer.

Lanza had joined Intel from Olivetti in the early seventies and was an important member of the microprocessor design group.

As far as I know, he was the designer of three fundamental chips for the MCS80 kit: the CRT Controller, the Disk Controller, and the DMA Controller.

I was told that at that meeting Intel would reveal to Olivetti some very sensitive industrial secrets under a Non-Disclosure Agreement and that for that reason they were taking advantage of Lanza's experience and his ability to speak the local language.

I later found that the meeting went quite well even if no real secrets were disclosed. The main announcement was the Intel plan to create software compatible CPUs in the future, as the "Crush Program" was specifying.

So, all in all, we had scored goals, thanks to our effort in Italy, and the Intel team and Mercurio met in December confirming their final decision in favor of Intel.

I did not delay a nanosecond to immediately inform Tom Lawrence, Ed Gelbach, and Jack Carsten, and we were all satisfied, too, because all that "working hard" had worked so well to conquer the great Olivetti.

But, as we know today, things did not end as we thought and the unpredictable had yet to happen.

The January 7th, 1980 Enrico Pesatori, Olivetti VP, invited me at lunch at Ivrea and during that lunch, he informed me that Olivetti changed mind and has chosen the Zilog Z8000 instead of the Intel 8086.

At the moment I thought I was dreaming; the whole great battle we had conducted was against Motorola and above all against their business size, their production capacity, etc. Never before Mercurio did send signals to me about the fact that Zilog was a risk.

Intel, Motorola, Zilog the three 16 bit contenders

I asked Pesatori the reason for that strange and sudden change of mind and he replied that Olivetti was very angry with Intel because Intel had publicized in the press in the US Olivetti's choice of 8086 without consent.

He also added that the choice had been made personally by President Carlo De Benedetti. Later, I made some personal inquiries to understand what had happened and I discovered that in reality, we had fallen into the personal war inside Olivetti, a war between Mercurio and other Olivetti managers that didn't accept the decision of his group. Having raised the level of the

Olivetti-Intel, failed joint venture

discussion that was previously at the technical level in our favor, the decision had turned into an internal political battle. The enemies of Mercurio had brought personally Federico Faggin to Italy to speak directly to Carlo De Benedetti and to SGS forcing them to promise that SGS would second sources the Z8000.

The Olivetti President Carlo De Benedetti, not involved in the technical choices, was placed in a position to choose a product that could be bought in Italy and chose the latter.

Nobody could at that point dare to oppose a President's decision, even Mercurio despite his position as a technical leader, and his decision was reversed.

Too bad for Olivetti, had they remained with the choice of Intel they would have reached the market many months before IBM with their PC. With the Z8000 Olivetti produced their first PC named M20, which was a commercial disaster and after a couple of years they were forced to copy the IBM PC branded M24 and forced to buy 8086 in large volume from Intel.

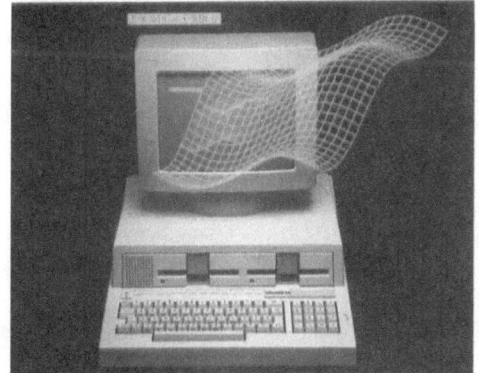

Con Zilog Z8000   Con Intel 8086

The two Olivetti's PCs

Olivetti Headquarters in Ivrea, Italy

Olivetti was founded as a typewriter manufacturer by Camillo Olivetti in 1908 in Ivrea, Italy. In the 1970s and 1980s, Olivetti was the biggest manufacturer for office machines in Europe and 2nd biggest PC vendor behind IBM in Europe.

In the year 1983 ATT, lacking computer expertise, sought a strategic alliance in Europe to gain instant access to distribution channels by purchasing 25% of Olivetti shares.

The Olivetti M24 rebadged AT&T PC 6300, was sold in the United State with great success: some 200,000 units were sold in 1986.

In late 1980s Olivetti's fortunes worsened stemmed from its troubled PC business has been late on several key innovations and lost its main partner ATT in 1989.

Olivetti had moved out of the typewriter business into personal computers before embracing telecoms between 1997 and 1999. In the process, it had lost around three-quarters of its staff.

In the 1990s, Olivetti's computer businesses were in great difficulty because of the competition. It was on the brink of collapse and had needed government support to stay afloat.

Olivetti-Intel failed joint venture

In this chapter, I wish to discuss an important operation which I conducted between 1984 and 1985 and which has remained secret until now.

During these years the American semiconductor producers were in crisis, mainly due to Japanese competition.

Even Intel was suffering and Robert Noyce was able to involve the Government to introduce special customs duties against the invasion of Japanese products.

At the same time, Semantech was founded, a consortium of American manufacturers to combine many resources to fight against the Japanese producer. Robert Noyce was selected as president of Semantech.

At that same time, Olivetti had managed to create an important partnership with ATT in the US to manufacture computers and the appointed president of this ATT-Olivetti venture was Dr. Vittorio Cassoni.

This partnership provided a great prestige for Olivetti and Carlo De Benedetti in the US.

I knew Cassoni very well; we were university mate at the Polytechnic of Milan and he visited my family in Milan a couple of years before his move to New York.

For years I thought there should be a relationship between the Italian Olivetti and the American Intel, while the relationship between Intel and IBM seemed to be inappropriate. IBM was the world leader in large computers. Intel had little to do with this market while Olivetti was a world leader in small systems and had no component production capability unlike the IBM semiconductor design and production resources.

During a visit to Santa Clara in October 1985, speaking with Ed Gelbach and Jack Carsten I got the feeling that something was going wrong between Intel and IBM and asked if a talk between Olivetti and Intel about a possible partnership could be possible.

Ed Gelbach confirmed that he could talk about this subject with Olivetti and added that it must have been extremely reserved

I went to New York the November 25, 1985, and I proposed that I be the secret link between Intel and Carlo De Benedetti of whom he was a direct reporter.

27 Nov 1985. At Cassoni's home in New York

Cassoni liked the idea very much and told me that he would gladly meet Ed Gelbach to discuss the matter.

There was a continuous dialogue between Ed Gelbach, Cassoni, and myself. Ultimately Cassoni and I decided to secretly meet in New York Ed Gelbach.

```
26/02 23.20
 332332 ELEDRA I

VXY1021501-0404(0003/790)
TLX131 843332332
 SCI404 0003/790
 QU WDTLX
 843332332 332332
25FEB86/10:57
SC:789/0003/791

---U R G E N T---

TO: ETTORE ACCENTI
    ELEDRA
    20154 MILANO
    VIALE ELVEZIA, 18 ITALY
FR: ED GELBACH/SC6-42/X78172
    INTEL CORP/SANTA CLARA, CA

SUBJ: OLIVETTI MEETING

ETTORE,

THANK YOU FOR YOUR CALL ON FEBRUARY 19TH, IN REGARDS TO SETTING
UP A MEETING BETWEEN MYSELF AND OLIVETTI. BELOW ARE THE DATES
AND TIMES THAT WILL WORK FOR ME -- ALSO, LET ME KNOW IF YOU
WERE INTENDING TO HAVE A DINNER.

        POSSIBLE DATES FOR MTG:   THURSDAY, MARCH 6TH ==
                                  BETWEEN 12:00 AND 4:00 PM

                                  FRIDAY, MARCH 7TH
                                  BETWEEN 1:00 AND 3:00 PM

LET ME KNOW IF EITHER OF THESE TWO DATES WILL WORK FOR YOU.

REGARDS,
ED

        NOTE:   == THERE IS A POSSIBILITY THAT THIS DATE MAY NOT WORK --
                I WILL KNOW IN A DAY OR TWO AND WILL GET BACK
                TO YOU IMMEDIATELY, IF THERE IS A PROBLEM.

332332 ELEDRA I.....
SENT VIA ITT
```

The meeting took place in New York the March 1986 and there a visit of Cassoni to Santa Clara was agreed upon for the following month of April.

In the meantime, Ed Gelbach and I agreed to formalize my role in this delicate matter and Gelbach commissioned Bernard Giroud, then President of Intel Europe, to prepare a formal document specifying what my task was.

In particular, it was specified that I was dealing as a person and not as an administrator of my Eledra. I was to be paid the mandate legal fee of $ 8,000. Of course, not only did I not ask for any additional compensation, but would have refused any compensation if the objective could be achieved.

Here is the secret mandate that I still keep.

INTEL EUROPE · 1, RUE EDISON · BP 303 · 78054 St QUENTIN EN YVELINES CEDEX, FRANCE

Dott. Ing. Ettore Accenti
Corso Sempione, 20
20154 Milano
Italy

February 21, 1986

Dear Ettore,

As agreed during our February 20th telephone conversation, here is a description of your mission on behalf of Intel Corporation:

1. to create new conditions for rapid business expansion at Olivetti by means of top executive meetings between representatives of Intel and Olivetti.

2. a key milestone to be a meeting between Carlo de Benedetti and Andy Grove. Such a meeting should not happen later than July 31, 1986 and should create business opportunities with effect in 1986.

3. you are not authorized to act on Intel's behalf as its agent or to make commitments for Intel with respect to Olivetti except as provided above.

4. you will publish a monthly progress report addressed to Ed Gelbach and me no later than the first Friday of every month. Ed and I, and only them, will act as your Intel contacts during the mission.

5. you will receive a fixed fee of $8,000. Half ($4,000) to be paid immediately upon receipt of your invoice, the other half ($4,000) to be paid after successful completion of point 2 above. It will be at Intel's sole discretion to decide whether or not point 2 has been met.

   In addition Intel will pay all reasonable out-of-pocket expenses, including trips which have been approved in advance by me.

   All payments to be made against receipt of your invoice(s).

6. this mission is due to end on July 31, 1986 but Intel can revoke it at any time without explanation and with no further payment to be made except out-of-pocket expenses as described above.

7. by June 30, 1986 we will decide whether or not we will wish to have a follow on mission with terms and conditions to be agreed upon.

intel®

page two
B.Giroud

Feb.21'86

8. you will perform the above described mission in your individual capacity as an independent contractor and not in your capacity as a Director and Officer of Eledra.

9. you will keep all aspects of this mission strictly confidential.

Please will you acknowledge your agreement with the above terms by signing this letter where indicated below and returning a copy to me for my files.

Again thank you for your offer of cooperation. I sincerely hope it will have positive consequences on our relationship with Olivetti.

Best regards,

Bernard P. Giroud

cc: Ed Gelbach   Ettore Accenti

Olivetti-Intel, failed joint venture

On April 5, 1986, Gelbach confirmed to me that Noyce, Moore, and Grove were aware of this operation and that he had obtained from the green light to proceed to organize a meeting between Carlo De Benedetti and Andy Grove in Santa Clara by August 1986.

I had several talks with both Cassoni and Ed Gelbach and everything seemed to be proceeding in the direction of organizing the meeting between Carlo De Benedetti and Andy Grove as planned, but suddenly something happened.

I received a phone call from Cassoni on May 24, 1986, in which he told me that Ivrea was no longer willing to have the meeting and that he had to withdraw the agreement between De Benedetti and Grove to meet.

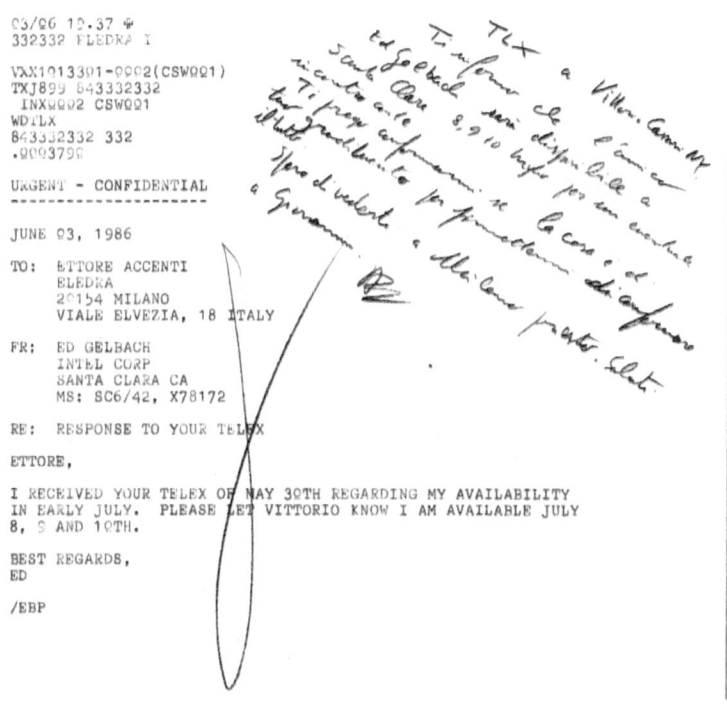

```
04/07 09.32
INTELCORP SNTA
+
332332 ELEDRA I
= =
DA ELEDRA SPA
05/0023815
03.07.1986
= =
 C.A. ED GELBACH
---
MILAN, JULY 3, 1986

TO : ED GELBACH - INTEL S.C.   MS: SC6/42, X78172

FM : ETTORE ACCENTI - ELEDRA

ED,
     VITTORIO WILL GET IN TOUCH WITH YOU DIRECTLY TO FIX A DAY
FOR YOUR MEETING.

MY BEST REGARDS.

ETTORE

INTELCORP SNTA
+
332332 ELEDRA I.....

0016_
```

Cassoni never confirmed to me whether it was Carlo De Benedetti himself who refused the meeting or others of his staff.

Cassoni died prematurely in 1991 and the only living person that might explain this mystery is Carlo De Benedetti.

Clearly, Olivetti and Italy lost another great opportunity here.

1991. Meeting with Dr. Gordon Moore and more

Even after my work with Intel, which ended the year 1987, I visited Silicon Valley many times and I went to see the Intel executives I worked with as if they were my old friends.

In 1991 I visited Silicon Valley with my whole family. I found a new building in Santa Clara dedicated to the memory of Robert Noyce who died prematurely the previous year.

Dr. Moore was extremely courteous and took us personally to visit the new building a much larger one compared to the one I was used to visiting on Bowers Avenue. He seemed very proud of this new earthquake-proof facility. With him, we even saw the rubber foundations to cushion the vibrations from earthquakes.

1991 – Visiting Gordon Moore, with my family

During lunch at the cafeteria, we talked about the future of integrated circuits and his law and he confessed that he too was amazed at what had happened and how production techniques had continued to refine semiconductor technology for decades.

My whole family appreciated that meeting and I think it will remain a vivid memory for them. We ended the tour of the new facilities, hoping to meet again soon.

With Jean Jones who organized my many visits to Intel

Beginning a tour at the white rooms

1993. From the 25th Intel event

intel®

July 3, 1991

Dear Ettori and Family,

Trust that you had a wonderful vacation and that you are now back home. Grand as a vacation can be, coming home is also good.

Enclosed are the items I promised to send.

It was very nice seeing you again and meeting your lovely family.

JEAN JONES

With Jean Jones who organized my many visits to Intel

The warm farewell with Gordon Moore

I documented that visit by taking up many photos copies of which I mailed to Gordon Moore. I can say that my children Emanuele, Edoardo, Elena, and Enrico enjoyed the opportunity to meet such an important people and to visit a amazing factory, a world that I had been part of during my life.

1991, Santa Clara visiting the Intel Museum

1991, Santa Clara, Intel Museum. Showing the 4004 microprocessor design group. From left Ted Hoff, Federico Faggin, Matsushita Shima, Stan Mazor

Palo Alto, 1980. Ed Gelbach on the left and Hank O'Hara on the right

1988 Santa Clara. Ed Gelbach and my wife Eva

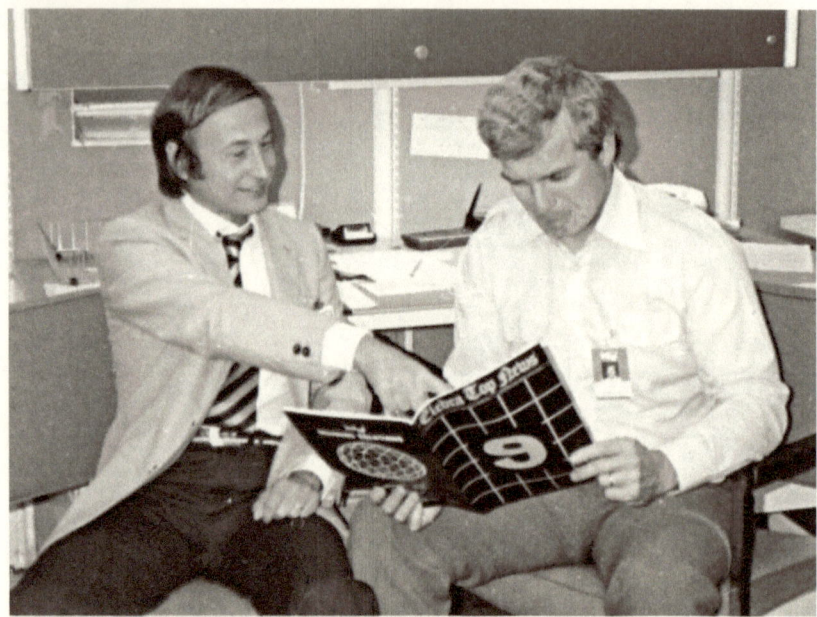
1980, Santa Clara. At Jack Carsten's office looking at his interview

1988 Los Altos. at Jack and Cassie home

1993. From the 25th Intel event

1985 Palo Alto. Dinner with Elvia and Federico Faggin

Palo Alto Chinese restaurant 10 years later

1988. Maurine and Stan Mazor home

2001 Maurine and Stan Mazor 4 years later

1993. From the 25th Intel event 175

1988. Sonia and Bill Davidow home

2008. Menlo Park with Bill Davidow after a tennis match

1993 - From the 25th Intel event

On the occasion of the twenty-fifth year since its birth, that is in the year 1993, Intel has released a beautiful album from which I could draw some of the historical images that follow. In particular, the album is summarized the most important events illustrated by year in conjunction with political events. This was a truly complete story that is worth re-reading here.

1 9 6 8

Memorable Movie:
The Graduate

FEBRUARY

Winter Olympic games held in Grenoble, France; Jean-Claude Killy and Peggy Fleming win gold medals.

APRIL

Martin Luther King, Jr. assassinated in Memphis, Tennessee.

Hair opens on Broadway.

JUNE

Senator Robert F. Kennedy assassinated in Los Angeles, California.

JULY

Bob Noyce and Gordon Moore incorporate new venture as N M Electronics; purchase rights to use Intel name from company using Intelco.

Arthur Rock is chairman of the Board; Bob Noyce is president and CEO; Gordon Moore is executive vice president.

AUGUST

Anti-Vietnam War riots mar Democratic National Convention in Chicago.

Company sets to work on Schottky TTL and silicon gate MOS technologies.

NOVEMBER

Nixon/Agnew defeat Humphrey/Muskie in presidential election.

1 9 6 9

Favorite TV Program:
Rowan & Martin's Laugh-In

Intel's 1968 revenues: $2,672.

FEBRUARY

Saturday Evening Post folds after 147 years.

MARCH

Intel opens office in Geneva, Switzerland.

APRIL

Intel introduces its first product, 3101 64-bit Schottky bipolar RAM.

JULY

During Apollo 11 mission, Neil Armstrong becomes first man to set foot on the moon.

Intel introduces the 1101, world's first MOS static RAM.

NOVEMBER

Brussels, Belgium office opens.

1970

Hit Song:
Bridge Over Troubled Water

JANUARY

Intel's 1969 revenues: $565,874.

Intel buys 26 acres in Santa Clara for first site purchase.

Beatles disband.

Millions celebrate first Earth Day.

MAY

Anti-war protest at Kent State University in Ohio; four students killed.

Intel opens sales and marketing in Japan.

JUNE

Recession forces company to lay off employees for first time.

OCTOBER

1103, world's first commercially successful DRAM, introduced.

1971

Popular Book:
Future Shock

JANUARY

Intel's 1970 revenues: $4,241,253.

APRIL

First U.S. visit to China since mid-1950s: ping-pong competition.

JUNE

U.S. voting age drops from 21 to 18.

Intel moves into its own building, Santa Clara 1 on Bowers Avenue.

JULY

Intel Paris opens.

AUGUST

Late List instituted.

SEPTEMBER

1702, world's first EPROM, introduced.

First $1-million month.

OCTOBER

Company goes public at $23.50* per share, raising $6.8 million.

NOVEMBER

Copenhagen, Denmark office opens.

4004, world's first microprocessor, introduced in *Electronic News* ad.

DECEMBER

Ms. magazine introduced.

*1 share in 1971 would be equivalent to 76 shares in 1993.

1973

Hit Song:
Tie a Yellow Ribbon 'Round the Old Oak Tree

JANUARY

Vietnam peace pact signed in Paris.

Intel's 1972 revenues: $23,417,000.

Assembly production begins at Penang, Malaysia's A1.

MARCH

Company orders custom-labeled bottles of champagne for employees to celebrate first $3-million month.

APRIL

Fab 3, Livermore, California opens. Bunny suits introduced.

Intel stock splits for first time, 3-for-2.

MAY

Four Nixon aides resign as Watergate scandal widens.

AUGUST

In London, doctors report use of first CAT scan.

Intellec 4-40 microprocessor development tool introduced.

OCTOBER

Arab nations impose oil embargo on U.S. and other Israel supporters.

1974

Popular Book:
The Joy of Sex

Favorite TV Program:
*M*A*S*H*

JANUARY

Intel's 1973 revenues: $66,170,000.

MARCH

A2, Manila, the Philippines opens.

APRIL

Hank Aaron hits 715th home run, surpassing Babe Ruth as the greatest slugger in baseball history.

Golda Meir resigns as Israel's Prime Minister.

JUNE

8080 industry-standard 8-bit microprocessor introduced.

JULY

House Judiciary Committee recommends three articles of impeachment against President Nixon.

Intel Israel (Haifa Design Center) opens.

AUGUST

Nixon resigns and Ford assumes U.S. presidency.

1975

Memorable Movie:
One Flew Over the Cuckoo's Nest

Popular Book:
Shogun

JANUARY
Intel's 1974 revenues: $134,456,000.

FEBRUARY
Intel's Stockholm, Sweden office opens.

MARCH
Intel introduces 8255 programmable peripheral interface.

ICE™-80, world's first in-circuit emulator, introduced.

APRIL
Bob Noyce elected chairman of the Board. Gordon Moore elected president and CEO.

MAY
Junko Tabei of Japan becomes first woman to reach summit of Mt. Everest.

140,000 South Vietnam refugees flown to U.S., following fall of Saigon.

Intel's original A1 building in Penang burns to the ground.

OCTOBER
MULTIBUS I specification introduced.

1976

Memorable Movie:
Rocky

JANUARY
Intel's 1975 revenues: $136,788,000.

Intel decides to proceed with development of the 8086 in addition to the iAPX 432.

FEBRUARY
Winter Olympic games held in Innsbruck, Austria. Dorothy Hamill wins gold in figure skating for the U.S.

APRIL
Intel Japan K.K. established.

MAY
iSBC® 80/10, first single-board computer, introduced.

JUNE
Company converts to 4-inch wafers.

JULY
U.S. celebrates bicentennial.

AUGUST
2147 static RAM, first HMOS product, introduced.

SEPTEMBER
Company opens facility in Santa Cruz.

OCTOBER
Aloha, Oregon site opens.

NOVEMBER
Carter/Mondale defeat Ford/Dole in presidential election.

8085 8-bit microprocessor introduced.

DECEMBER
8748/8048, world's first 8-bit microcontrollers, introduced.

1977

Favorite TV Program:
Happy Days

JANUARY
Intel's 1976 revenues: $225,979,000.

APRIL
Apple Computer introduces Apple II, a personal computer.

JUNE
Silver Jubilee for Queen Elizabeth II.
Intel opens Rotterdam, The Netherlands office.
Leonid Brezhnev becomes President of the Soviet Union.
Intel starts Penang, Malaysia's T3.

AUGUST
Volkswagen phases out "Bug" in U.S.
Intel hires 10,000th employee.

SEPTEMBER
First *Inteleads* published.
Intel's Oslo, Norway office opens.
2910, first single-chip codec, introduced.
Intel enters bubble memory business.

OCTOBER
Barbados, West Indies site opens.

NOVEMBER
Egypt's Anwar Sadat makes historic first visit to Israel

1978

Hit Song:
Stayin' Alive

JANUARY
Intel's 1977 revenues: $282,549,000.
8041/8741 universal peripheral interface introduced.

MARCH
Intel opens Helsinki, Finland office.

APRIL
Intel phases out of the Microma digital watch business.
Intel's Hannover, Stuttgart and Wiesbaden, West Germany offices open.

JUNE
8086 industry-standard 16-bit microprocessor introduced.
Preview magazine debuts; renamed *Solutions* in 1981, *Microcomputer Solutions* in 1987, *Intel Solutions* in 1993.

JULY
Louise Brown, world's first test-tube baby, born in London.
iRMX® 80 operating system introduced.
Intel's Hawthorn Farms, Oregon opens.

AUGUST
Intel marks 10th anniversary with celebration at Cow Palace in San Francisco, California.

OCTOBER
Poland's John Paul II named Pope.
Fab 5, Aloha, Oregon opens.

DECEMBER
Israel's Begin and Egypt's Sadat jointly win Nobel Peace Prize.

1979

Memorable Movie:
Apocalypse Now

JANUARY
Intel's 1978 revenues: $399,390,000.
Intel opens office in Milan, Italy.

FEBRUARY
Intel's Zurich, Switzerland office opens.

MARCH
Bob Noyce receives IEEE Faraday Medal.

APRIL
Gordon Moore elected chairman of the Board; Bob Noyce elected vice chairman; Andy Grove elected president and COO.

MAY
Margaret Thatcher selected Great Britain's first woman Prime Minister.
8088 industry-standard 8-bit microprocessor introduced.
Intel makes Fortune 500 list: No. 486.
Intel introduces the FAST-3805 Semiconductor Disk Unit.

JUNE
Intel Magnetics introduces first product: 1-megabit bubble memory.
Hillsboro, Oregon site opens.

OCTOBER
Intel opens office in Sydney, Australia.

NOVEMBER
Bob Noyce awarded National Medal of Science by President Jimmy Carter.

1980

Favorite TV Program:
Dallas

JANUARY
Intel's 1979 revenues: $660,984,000.
Intel Semiconductor, Ltd., Hong Kong opens its doors.

FEBRUARY
STAR order processing system installed.

JUNE
Intel introduces the first math coprocessor, the 8087.

APRIL
Bob Noyce elected to the National Academy of Sciences.

MAY
Intel, DEC and Xerox join forces to develop Ethernet.
Solidarity Union formed in Gdansk; Lech Walesa, leader.
Intel and Ford Motor Corporation complete development of 8061 and 8361 two-chip electronic engine control system.
P2 opens in Las Piedras, Puerto Rico.

NOVEMBER
Reagan/Bush defeat Carter/Mondale in presidential election.

DECEMBER
Dun's Review names Intel one of America's five best-managed companies.
Intel closes first fab in Mountain View.

1981

Hit Song:
Bette Davis Eyes

Popular Book:
A Woman of Substance

Favorite TV Program:
Little House on the Prairie

JANUARY

Intel's 1980 revenues: $854,561,000.
Fab 7, Rio Rancho, New Mexico opens.

FEBRUARY

iAPX 432 microprocessor introduced.

MARCH

President Reagan shot and wounded in Washington, D.C.

JULY

Britain's Prince Charles weds Lady Diana Spencer.

Intel opens in Swindon, U.K.
Intel's sabbatical program begins in U.S.
IBM announces its first PC, based on Intel's 8088 microprocessor.

SEPTEMBER

France starts service on bullet train between Paris and Lyons.

Bob Noyce becomes chairman of Semiconductor Industry Association.

OCTOBER

Egyptian leader Anwar Sadat assassinated.

Intel's "125% Solution" launched.

NOVEMBER

Intel introduces System 86/330. Groundbreaking for Fab 8 in Jerusalem, Israel.

DECEMBER

Scientists identify a new disease: AIDS.

1982

Memorable Movie:
E.T. The Extra-Terrestrial

JANUARY

Intel's 1981 revenues: $788,676,000.

FEBRUARY

Intel and AMD enter microprocessor peripheral exchange agreement.

MARCH

AT&T break-up announced.

80186/188 high-integration 16-bit embedded processors introduced.
80286 high-performance 16-bit microprocessor introduced.
First LAN coprocessor, the 82586, introduced.
2914, first combo codec/filter chip, introduced.

APRIL

Argentina invades Falkland Islands.

P3, Puerto Rico, opens.

MAY

U.S. Equal Rights Amendment defeated.

AUGUST

8096, first 16-bit microcontroller, introduced.

SEPTEMBER

Wall Street Transcript names Gordon Moore the outstanding CEO for the semiconductor industry the second year in a row.

OCTOBER

7114 4-Mbit bubble memory introduced.

NOVEMBER

CEAMS (Component Engineering Analysis and Manufacturing System) tracking system for wafer fabrication introduced.

DECEMBER

Dr. Barney Clark receives first permanent artificial heart.

IBM announces plans to purchase 12% of Intel for $250 million.

1993. From the 25th Intel event

1983

Popular Book:
Real Men Don't Eat Quiche

JANUARY

Intel's 1982 revenues: $899,812,000.

Intel imposes pay freeze/salary cuts in face of continuing poor business conditions.

80C51 and 80C49, CHMOS versions of 8051 and 8049, introduced.

Inteleads publishes first April Fool's issue.

MAY

Madrid, Spain office opens.

JUNE

Sally Ride is first American woman astronaut on space shuttle Challenger.

OCTOBER

241 U.S. Marines and sailors, 40 French paratroopers killed in terrorist bombing in Lebanon.

American troops defeat Cuban forces on Grenada.

Europeans protest U.S. deployment of missiles in Europe.

NOVEMBER

I²ICE system introduced.

Intel builds first wafer containing 25 million bits of information.

DECEMBER

Fab 7 achieves first functional die on 150mm (6-inch) wafers.

1984

Memorable Movie:
Ghostbusters

JANUARY

Apple introduces the Macintosh personal computer.

Intel passes the $1-billion annual revenue mark, announcing 1983 revenues of $1,121,943,000.

FEBRUARY

Winter Olympic games held in Sarajevo, Yugoslavia.

MARCH

Gordon Moore and Bob Noyce named to IEEE Hall of Fame.

MAY

Intel chosen one of "100 Best Companies to Work For" in book of same name.

JUNE

Intel Singapore opens.

JULY

Geraldine Ferraro becomes first woman to run for U.S. vice president on a major party ticket.

AUGUST

IBM announces PC AT,* based on Intel's 80286 microprocessor.

OCTOBER

U.S. Congress passes landmark Semiconductor Chip Protection Act.

Fortune magazine highlights Intel as one of eight masters of innovation.

NOVEMBER

Vietnam Memorial unveiled in Washington, D.C.

Reagan/Bush defeat Mondale/Ferraro in presidential election.

DECEMBER

South Africa's Bishop Desmond Tutu awarded Nobel Peace Prize.

Intel announces closing of operations in Austin, Texas.

PCEO (Personal Computer Enhancement Operation) starts Intel PC retail sales.

NEC sues Intel, seeking to show microcode is not copyrightable.

1985

Favorite TV Program:
The Cosby Show

JANUARY

Intel's 1984 revenues: $1,629,332,000.

Intel Technology Asia Ltd. opens office in Seoul, Korea.

FEBRUARY

U.S./Japan agree to eliminate tariffs on importation of semiconductors.

iPSC® Supercomputer unveiled.

Intel announces first layoffs in 10 years and plans to close T2 in Santa Cruz and A0 in Santa Clara.

MARCH

OpenNET local area network introduced.

APRIL

Intel ranked 226th in Fortune 500.

ABOVE™ board products introduced.

Intel Taipei, Taiwan office opens.

MAY

Intel's French headquarters open in Saint-Quentin-en-Yvelines.

AUGUST

Intel opens Folsom, California site.

SEPTEMBER

Huge earthquake kills thousands in Mexico City.

Divers find wreck of the Titanic— 73 years after it sank in Atlantic Ocean.

Intel/AMD/National Semiconductor file joint anti-dumping petition with U.S. Government against Japanese EPROM manufacturers.

OCTOBER

Intel decides to quit the DRAM business.

Intel386™ CPU introduced in San Francisco, London, Paris, Munich and Tokyo.

DECEMBER

Bob Noyce inducted into National Inventors Hall of Fame.

Intel opens Beijing office in China.

1986

Hit Song:
That's What Friends Are For

Favorite TV Program:
Miami Vice

JANUARY

Space shuttle Challenger explodes moments after lift-off, killing 7 aboard.

Intel's 1985 revenues: $1,364,982,000.

Asia Pacific Operation formed.

FEBRUARY

20-year rule of Philippines President Ferdinand Marcos ends.

Flexible Workforce Program introduced.

APRIL

Major accident at Chernobyl nuclear reactor power plant in Ukraine.

Fab 6 introduces GORE-TEX® bunny suits.

MAY

82786 graphics coprocessor unveiled.

JULY

U.S. and Japan sign historic semiconductor accord designed to increase U.S. market share in Japan.

Martina Navratilova wins 5th straight women's Wimbledon tennis title.

Intel System 310s track information in Operation Sail 1986 at the 100th anniversary Salute to Liberty in New York.

AUGUST

Intel announces plans to shut down Barbados facility.

29C53 transceiver chip and 29C48 codec filter combo chip, Intel's first ISDN products, introduced.

As part of Intel/NEC dispute, court rules that microcode can be copyrighted and that Intel's copyright is valid.

Compaq is first major computer maker to introduce an Intel386™ CPU-based PC.

OCTOBER

Intel announces entry into ASIC market.

NOVEMBER

Iran-Contra affair becomes full-fledged scandal for Reagan administration.

DECEMBER

Experimental U.S. aircraft, Voyager, circles the earth nonstop on one tank of gas.

Electronic Engineering Times readers select the Intel386™ CPU as the most significant IC product of the year.

1987

Memorable Movie:
Fatal Attraction

Hit Song:
Didn't We Almost Have It All?

JANUARY

Dow Jones Industrial Average tops the 2,000 mark for first time.

Intel's 1986 revenues: $1,265,011,000.

APRIL

After 1986 net loss, Intel celebrates first-quarter net income of $25,511,000. Employees worldwide celebrate with "Back in the Black" parties.

Andy Grove elected CEO.

MAY

SIA Board of Directors approves business plan for SEMATECH.

Intel's Systems Group World Headquarters opens at Hawthorn Farms, Oregon.

JUNE

Bob Noyce receives National Medal of Technology from President Reagan.

Andy Grove receives 1987 Engineering Leadership Recognition award from IEEE.

Intel repurchases the shares of Intel stock sold to IBM in 1983.

Intel Brazil opens in Sao Paulo.

JULY

Intel386™ CPU-based System 301 introduced.

AUGUST

National Semiconductor announces plans to buy Fairchild Semiconductor.

SEPTEMBER

Intel launches Knockout campaign.

OCTOBER

Dow Jones Industrial Average plummets 508 points, or 22.6 percent, in one day.

D1 development fab for microprocessors opens in Aloha, Oregon.

DECEMBER

IBM sells the last of its shares of Intel stock, closing out its stake in the company.

1988

Memorable Movie:
Big

JANUARY

Intel's 1987 revenues: $1,907,105,000.
Intel's domestic facilities go "smokeless."
Employee Cash Bonus announced.

FEBRUARY

Intel Asia Electronics opens in India.

MARCH

Superman turns 50.

Intel stock listed for first time on Swiss Stock Exchanges.

APRIL

The Big Bang–16 new products and development tools designed for embedded control applications–introduced.

JUNE

NASA report reveals that global temperatures have risen, creating the "greenhouse effect."

Intel and Siemens announce BiiN joint venture.

Intel announces it will build employee showers in most U.S. sites.

Late List ends.

Intel Foundation established.

JULY

Bob Noyce accepts position as SEMATECH CEO.

OCTOBER

Intel acquires DVI® (Digital Video Interactive) technology from General Electric/RCA, opens Intel Princeton (New Jersey) Operation.

Intel opens new Munich I facility in Feldkirchen, Germany.

Intel embarks on joint venture with the People's Republic of China to manufacture 16- and 32-bit microcomputers.

NOVEMBER

Bush/Quayle defeat Dukakis/Bentsen in U.S. presidential election.

1989

Popular Book:
*All I Really Need to Know
I Learned in Kindergarten*

JANUARY

Japan's Emperor Hirohito dies at 87.

Intel's 1988 revenues: $2,874,769,000.

FEBRUARY

Barbie celebrates her 30th birthday.

Intel and AT&T Microelectronics announce five-year product and technology exchange.

Final judgment on Intel and NEC dispute rules that microcode is protected under copyright laws.

i860™ processor introduced at the Uniforum scientific computing trade show.

MARCH

Exxon Valdez tanker runs aground on Alaska coast, spilling 240,000 barrels of oil.

APRIL

1.2 million-transistor Intel486™ processor introduced.

JUNE

Iran's Ayatollah Khomeini dies.

Thousands of protesters killed by Chinese soldiers in Tienanmen Square, Beijing, China.

SEPTEMBER

Intel introduces i960® CA processor for embedded applications.

Intel Foundation announces its first graduate fellowships.

Intel's site in Las Piedras, Puerto Rico suffers little damage from Hurricane Hugo.

OCTOBER

An earthquake measuring 7.1 on the Richter scale hits the San Francisco Bay area.

Intel and Siemens AG agree to sell BiiN.

Intel announces plans to build systems manufacturing plant and a fab in Leixlip, Ireland.

Bob Noyce and Jack Kilby share the National Academy of Engineering's first Charles Stark Draper prize for the co-invention of the integrated circuit.

NOVEMBER

Berlin Wall crumbles as East Germany opens its borders.

1990

Memorable Movie:
Dances with Wolves

JANUARY

Intel's 1989 revenues: $3,126,833,000.

Craig Barrett becomes executive vice president of Intel, joining chairman Gordon Moore and president and CEO Andy Grove in the executive office.

FEBRUARY

Black Nationalist leader Nelson Mandela freed after 27 years in a South African prison.

MAY

Intel Foundation funds "Information Age: People, Information and Technology" at Smithsonian Institution, Washington, D.C.

A team of five design engineers from Intel's Haifa Design Center win Israel's Rothschild prize for their work on 8087 and Intel387™ math coprocessors.

Gordon Moore elected a Fellow of the American Academy of Arts and Sciences.

JUNE

Malaysia's royal couple visits Intel's site in Penang.

Bob Noyce, Intel vice chairman and co-founder, dies.

AUGUST

Iraq invades Kuwait.

SEPTEMBER

Intel is named the first semiconductor supplier to win Ford's Total Quality Excellence Award.

OCTOBER

Intel announces establishment of annual Intel Quality Awards.

Intel's first billion-dollar quarter.

NOVEMBER

Gordon Moore receives the National Medal of Technology from President George Bush.

DECEMBER

Intel Penang named winner of 1990 Prime Minister's Award for Quality.

1993. From the 25th Intel event

1991

Hit Song:
Unforgettable

JANUARY

Intel's 1990 revenues: $3,921,274,000.

Intel Foundation establishes the Robert Noyce Memorial Fellowship fund.

FEBRUARY

Operation Desert Storm vs. Iraq.

APRIL

Intel's Dov Frohman awarded the annual Israel Prize in Engineering.

Fab 1 in Santa Clara shuts down.

Intel announces it will cease further development of the EPROM in favor of flash memory development.

MAY

Intel launches Intel Inside® program.

Intel's Touchstone Delta system, then the fastest supercomputer in the world, is dedicated at the California Institute of Technology.

JUNE

Croatia and Slovenia declare independence from Yugoslavia; Serbo-Croat battles erupt.

AUGUST

The site in Palo Alto, California where Bob Noyce invented the integrated circuit becomes California's 1,000th historic landmark.

SEPTEMBER

Baltic republics gain independence from USSR.

Fab 3 closes in Livermore, California.

Intel introduces 23 new networking products.

OCTOBER

At COMDEX, Andy Grove introduces the concept of computer-supported collaboration with demonstration.

NOVEMBER

L.A. Lakers superstar Earvin "Magic" Johnson announces he tested HIV positive.

Intel launches "Vacancy" commercial on prime-time television.

Intel and IBM establish Robert N. Noyce Development Center.

Supercomputer Systems Division announces the Paragon™ XP/S supercomputer.

DECEMBER

Soviet Union disbands and is replaced by Commonwealth of Independent States.

Intel opens sales office in Moscow.

1992

Favorite TV Program:
Murphy Brown

JANUARY

Intel's 1991 revenues: $4,778,616,000.

FEBRUARY

In arbitration, Judge rules AMD is not entitled to the Intel386™ microprocessor under an earlier second-source agreement, but he awards the right to sell its copy of the Intel386 CPU.

MARCH

Intel announces InerDrive™ processors.

APRIL

Intel's D2 Fab in Santa Clara produces first 8-inch wafers.

In-Stat names Intel world's largest maker of ICs, passes NEC.

JUNE

Jury rules that AMD has no right to copy the Intel287™ math coprocessor microcode.

SEPTEMBER

Intel announces 10-cents-per-share payout (before effect of May 1993 stock split), first cash dividend in the company's history.

Intel opens D1A in Aloha, Oregon.

OCTOBER

Intel announces a $400 million expansion of D2 manufacturing plant.

Clinton/Gore defeat Bush/Quayle in the presidential election.

Intel introduces Indeo™ video technology.

Intel opens office in Guadalajara, Mexico.

Intel establishes Penang Design Center.

DECEMBER

European Community becomes a reality as trade borders disappear.

Court rules that AMD does not have the right to copy any Intel microcode.

Conclusion

My long collaboration between the electronic industry in Silicon Valley and Italy leads me to say how those two environments, Italy and California, were the basis of great diversity and certainly not individual skills.

I have seen Italian immigrants from Italy quickly become great, successful, entrepreneurs such as Faggin, Cafiero, Torresi, Lanza, and Mazzola and create economic fortunes unattainable in Italy.

I have collaborated on the success of companies that we admire from our country but whose founders were not necessarily superior to people such as Olivetti's Perotto, Vinsani, and Mercurio, just to mention some of the dozens I knew and worked with.

Perhaps the best way to give perspective is from an old guide that I picked up at Palo Alto in 1984, the "Rich's Business Guide of Silicon Valley", which illustrates the environment better than most.

"Silicon Valley is the largest concentration of Hi-Tech companies in the world. The nature of this industry creates continuous changes not only for the state of the art but also for the location of the companies, their configuration, and the products of these entrepreneurs, artists of technology. In the course of one night, giants are born, companies merge, companies become public and many people become millionaires in a moment. Some people leave their employers and open other small companies, hoping to find the magic of new products and services; some succeed, others fail and the search for success and wealth begins again. This exciting and innovative climate, which accepts both success and failure with respect, is largely the reason for US leadership in the Hi-Tec world."

I believe that this free and competitive spirit is not found anywhere in other countries and can hardly be created artificially.

My only regret is these great entrepreneurial immigrants from Italy, once they have achieved their incredible successes, have not built anything in their native country, and return only for a holiday.

www.ingramcontent.com/pod-product-compliance
Lightning Source LLC
Chambersburg PA
CBHW020653220526
45464CB00001B/412